FABIAN
INTERNATIONAL ESSAYS

FABIAN INTERNATIONAL ESSAYS

Edited by
T. E. M. McKITTERICK
and
KENNETH YOUNGER

PRAEGER

NEW YORK

First Published in the United States in 1957
by
Frederick A. Praeger, Inc., Publishers
150 East 52nd Street, New York 22, N.Y.

Library of Congress Catalog Card Number 57-6288

Preface

THESE Essays on International Affairs fully maintain the high standard set by earlier, similar publications of the Fabian Society. Although they are a collection of individual contributions and do not present to the reader a consistent theme or policy throughout, they cover between them most of the major issues of world affairs today. Their approach is objective and realistic. This is especially to be desired in a field where perhaps more than in any other illusions of one kind or another are apt to persist and ideas are so swiftly outdated by events.

I am sure that this book will be welcomed as a most valuable guide through the complexities of international problems and as an excellent stimulant to thought and discussion on these matters within the Labour Movement.

August, 1956   Hugh Gaitskell

Note on Contributors

RICHARD LOWENTHAL is Foreign Affairs Commentator of the *Observer*.

THOMAS BALOGH is a Fellow of Balliol College, Oxford.

JOHN STRACHEY is Member of Parliament for Dundee West and was Secretary of State for War 1950–51.

T. E. M. McKITTERICK is Chairman of the Fabian International Bureau.

KENNETH YOUNGER is Member of Parliament for Grimsby and was Minister of State for Foreign Affairs 1950–51.

P. C. GORDON WALKER is Member of Parliament for Smethwick and was Secretary of State for Commonwealth Relations 1950–51.

DENIS HEALEY is Member of Parliament for Leeds East and was Secretary, International Department, the Labour Party 1945–52.

Contents

Editors' Note

THE essays in this book were written over a period of months at the end of 1955 and early in 1956 and went to press in May 1956. Only a minimum of revision took place after that date. For instance, as a footnote on page 107 indicates, it was not possible to take account of the events which followed President Nasser's nationalisation of the Suez Canal. But this does not affect the essays materially because they deal mainly with longer-term issues.

The views expressed by each author are his own and not those of the Fabian Society or necessarily of the editor.

I

CO-EXISTENCE WITH SOVIET COMMUNISM

RICHARD LOWENTHAL

CAN Soviet communism and the non-communist world in the long run live side by side without clashing in a disastrous war? Nowadays almost everybody agrees that this is the life and death question of international politics. Yet that in itself is only a fairly recent development. True, the question is as old as the Bolshevik revolution in Russia—little short of 40 years—but few people worried about it in the twenties, and only Hitler and his associates regarded it as a serious problem in the thirties. Thus if we wish to understand the meaning of the question in its actual context of present-day power politics, as distinct from its place, say, in a history of Communist doctrine, we had better start by asking what has given it this immense topical urgency.

The answer, I think, is threefold. First, Hitler's war and Hitler's defeat by a coalition of the western powers and the Soviet Union led to a situation where the latter became the predominant military power in the whole of Eastern Europe up to the Elbe, and the occupying power in most of this territory; and between 1944 and 1948 this military predominance was used by the Soviet leaders to impose communist one-party régimes, modelled on their own system and controlled by it through party ties, on this entire area, excepting only Finland and the Russian zone of Austria. Moreover, the long-drawn-out civil war in China ended in 1949 with the total victory of the Chinese communists and the establishment of their 'Chinese People's Republic'. As a result of these two developments, centralised communist parties imbued with a single doctrine and regarding themselves as parts of a single 'camp' in world politics—a camp having its centre and supreme leadership in the Soviet Union—have come to exercise complete totalitarian control over a huge continuous area inhabited by 900 million people, including the two dominant military powers of the Eurasian continent. The communist bloc, irrespective of its actual intentions, has thus objectively become what the Soviet Union had never been between the wars—a potential contender for supreme world power.

Second, this tremendous advance in the power of Soviet communism has been achieved largely by the use or threat of military force—chiefly home-grown force in the case of China, chiefly foreign (i.e. Russian) force in the cases of Eastern Europe and North Korea. It has been partly accompanied, partly followed by unsuccessful attempts to use force or the threat of force for similar purposes elsewhere—e.g. the attempt to set up a communist government in Persian Azerbaijan during the Russian post-war occupation, the attempt to overthrow the Greek government by the formation of a partisan army supported by Greece's communist neighbours in 1947-9, the attempt to end democratic self-government in Berlin and to force a withdrawal of the western powers from the city by the blockade in 1948-9, and the attempt to extend the communist regime of North Korea by military conquest to South Korea after the withdrawal of the Americans in 1950. Between them, these successful and unsuccessful acts of forcible communist expansion have led to the creation of a system of military alliances of non-communist states under American leadership, to the establishment of a chain of military bases around the periphery of the communist bloc, and to an intense and costly armaments race. Not only the existence of a communist and a non-communist camp in world politics, but the existence of acute military tension between them involving ultimately the danger of world war, has thus entered the general consciousness.

The third and decisive factor accounting for the urgency of the problem of co-existence is, of course, the development of atomic and thermo-nuclear weapons by both sides. The destructive potentialities, horrible enough in the case of the 'ordinary' atomic bomb, are by now practically unlimited for hydrogen bombs; yet despite all efforts to work out schemes for a ban on weapons of mass destruction, it is now generally admitted by experts that such a ban could not be effectively controlled, and hence has no chance of acceptance in a state of profound mutual distrust between two hostile blocs. The conclusion is that there can be no reasonable guarantee against the use of these weapons in case of another world war, i.e. a war in which the balance of world power is at stake. The chances of the survival of mankind are therefore largely identical with the prospects of avoiding a third world war; and as such a world war at present seems only conceivable between the communist and non-communist camps, it follows that the survival of mankind may depend on the success of 'co-existence'.

It is in the light of these three factors—the actual power relations in the post-war world, the causes of the formation of opposed military blocs, and the technological threat of total destruction in case of a third world war—that the conditions of co-existence with Soviet Communism must be examined. There are, of course, some happy optimists who think that the problem has already been solved by recent changes in the Soviet Union—changes affecting important features of the internal *régime*, such as the political power of the secret police and the labour camp system, as well as the international doctrine and practice of the Soviet Communist party. I am far from belittling these changes and will discuss some of them in the course of this essay; yet at this stage it is sufficient to point out that in the view of the Soviet Communist leaders themselves, as expressed in the speeches and resolutions of the Twentieth Party Congress, they do not eliminate the division of the world into two opposed 'camps' and the problem of their co-existence, but merely offer new possibilities for its solution.

In fact the very word co-existence, coined by Lenin and his associates during the effort at consolidation which followed their victory in the Russian civil war, forms part of a coherent communist doctrine whose continuity of development—under Lenin and Stalin, as now under Khrushchev—the Soviet leaders proudly emphasise today: a doctrine that purports to explain the character of the two contending sides, the nature of the conflict between them, and the policies likely to reduce the threat of a disastrous clash. It will therefore be a convenient approach to our problem to take first of all a critical look at this Communist theory of co-existence.

In the Soviet communist view, the international conflict now dividing the world is an aspect of the class struggle between the working class and their capitalist exploiters, or between a rising, socialist form of economic and social organisation and a declining, capitalist one. The states of the Soviet bloc, according to that theory, are countries in which the workers under the leadership of the Communist Party have seized state power and are successfully using it for the socialist and ultimately communist transformation of society; everywhere else, state power is still in the hands of a capitalist class of private owners of the means of production—either of native capitalists or those of one of the great imperialist powers—and is used to maintain the system of capitalist exploitation in its present phase of imperialist decline. This system, however, is increasingly suffering from its inherent contradictions—from the class conflicts between workers and exploiters within the advanced imperialist nations, from the rivalries among the imperialist powers in their struggle for markets and raw materials, and from the anti-imperialist liberation movements of the exploited colonial and semi-colonial nations. As a result of these contradictions, the territory controlled by the imperialists is inevitably shrinking as their rule is overthrown by revolutions in one country after another, while the territory controlled by the communists is inevitably expanding; it follows that the communists have no need to precipitate a decision in this struggle by embarking on the adventure of world war, but that the most class-conscious imperialists must wish to launch such a war in order to destroy the communist menace once for all while they are still strong enough. The tendency towards world war is therefore inherent in the situation, but the plans of the warmongers may be foiled at any given moment by skilful exploitation of the internal rivalries among them and by mobilisation of the people in their own countries who are longing for peace; the ultimate clash may thus be postponed again and again, possibly until the imperialists no longer have the strength to risk it.

This communist doctrine, first formulated under Lenin, has never been abandoned under Stalin, and has lately been reaffirmed by Khrushchev with greater emphasis on the prospect of ultimately avoiding world war. In essence the doctrine does not depend on the horrors of the H-bomb; even during its most aggressive phases, Russian policy has consciously sought to avoid the risk of world war. But neither is even the latest optimistic version based on any hope that 'peaceful co-existence' would lead to a gradual softening of the conflict between the two camps; on the contrary, it is part of the doctrine of co-existence that this conflict is irreconcilable. 'Peace', in this context, merely means the avoidance of world war; and that is sought for as the most favourable condition for the gradual expansion and the ultimate victory of communism—whether by peaceful or by violent means.*

The doctrine I have sketched out is believed in by the communist rulers as an essential part of the general theory and strategy of Leninism by which they seek to orient their practical political action; it is therefore of great importance as a clue for understanding that action, quite independent of its inherent truth or falsehood. But we have now to turn to a critical examination of it in order to lay a secure foundation for our own action.

II

THE first assumption we must question is the description of the Soviet bloc as an area of 'workers' rule', or of 'socialist construction'. I do not wish to engage in a futile dispute as to what constitutes the 'true' definition of socialism; we accept as a starting point the Marxist criterion from which the communists,

*The fact that for the communists 'peaceful co-existence' means a form of irreconcilable conflict is often obscured because the behaviour of communist governments, both in words and in deeds, may vary widely in different phases of the conflict. During a phase of communist expansion, as we have seen, force and the threat of force may be used freely, limited only by the desire to avoid the supreme risk of world war; during a phase of consolidation, such as we are experiencing now, offers of disarmament and pacts of non-aggression take the place of military threats. The change is a real and important one, not a mere pretence; but it is a change in the means employed and in the immediate objectives pursued in the world conflict, not in the fundamental antagonism itself. If we wish to reserve the term 'cold war' for the former policy of threats and abuse, we may say that the cold war has ended; but that statement will be dangerously misleading unless we add at once that the present policy of 'peaceful co-esistence' is the continuation of the cold war by different means.

too, have started—that the aim of all socialists is to end the private control of economic life by a privileged class based on the private ownership of the means of production, and to replace it by social control. In the countries of communist rule, private control of economic life and private ownership of the principal means of production have certainly been abolished, but they have been replaced by the ownership of an all-powerful state whose machine is not subject to any form of control by society, and is run by a dictatorial party which is truly above society. The communists, of course, assert that their monopolistic party 'represents' the working class, or indeed all the productive classes of Soviet society—workers, peasants and 'intelligentsia'—but they have for 35 years persistently refused to put this fiction to the test by offering their people alternative means of information outside the official propaganda, alternative forms of organisation outside those controlled by the official party, or a choice of alternative policies—either inside or outside that party. The recent decision to end the 'new look' drive for a higher share of consumer goods in total production and to restore the primacy of heavy industry was not taken by the working people of the Soviet Union; like every other decision under the communist regime, it was taken over their heads by a handful of leaders. Mr. Aneurin Bevan has defined socialism as a system of democratic decision about priorities; in that essential sense, which is nothing but a reformulation in modern terms of the classical Marxist concept, the Soviet system, after almost forty years, is as remote from socialism as ever. Yet the identical system has been imposed, without any change, on the more advanced countries of eastern and central Europe which were conquered for 'communism' by the Russian army.

Under this system, economic power, and with it economic privilege, have indeed been taken from the old class of private owners, but they have been vested not in the people, who lack all democratic means of control, but in a new class of state and party bureaucrats. Yet this new privileged class has not so far been allowed to become a conservative force; for it has received its position from the hands of the ruling totalitarian party, and that party has sought to prove the need for its continual dictatorship by imposing ever new revolutionary changes on a society whose productive classes have no organs of self-defence. Thus the first revolution was followed in Russia—and is now being followed in China—by the 'second revolution' of a forced collectivisation, imposed from above; and the outlines of a third revolution transforming the collective farmers into state workers receiving wages on a piece-rate system are dimly beginning to take shape before our eyes as Mr. Khrushchev gets into his stride. All this is being justified, of course, by the need to complete 'socialism' and to prepare the 'transition to communism'; but it means no approach to social control, only more and more complete domination over every aspect of life by the one-party state.

There have, it is true, been some hopeful signs at the twentieth congress of the Soviet Communist Party that the régime may find it necessary to slow down this process of permanent revolution and to humanise its methods: this, at least, would seem to be the implicit meaning of the rejection of the last twenty years of Stalinist practice. But however welcome such a change would be, it would still leave both the power monopoly of the party and the economic privileges of the bureaucracy intact, and the masses of the people without any share in controlling their destiny. Such is the totalitarian system that has been expanding with every success of the Soviet bloc.

What, then, about the second assumption of the Soviet doctrine of co-existence—that the non-communist world is dominated by the capitalist classes of the imperialist powers, and is incapable of overcoming the contradictions of the capitalist system in its decline? Obviously the non-communist world includes the powerful capitalist groups of the west; but it also includes strong democratic labour movements, who have already succeeded in greatly transforming the economic and social structure of the advanced industrial countries. The British Labour movement would not claim that the achievement of recognised state responsibility for full employment, of the welfare state and the nationalisation of some of Britain's key industries have already made this a socialist country. But they evidently constitute vital steps forward along the road of socialist transformation, which leads to effective control of the use of the nation's resources by democratic methods. Nor could it be denied that the American trade unions, who do not call themselves socialist, have had a considerable impact on the functioning of the American economy both by direct union action and by their backing of the New Deal reforms, or that American and European labour influence together has helped to transform international economic relations within the western world by its backing of the Marshall Plan.

So far from being undermined by the class struggle until they are ripe for communist revolution, the advanced capitalist countries are thus evolving, in different forms and at different paces, with pauses and setbacks, but none the less recognisably, along the road of democratic socialist transformation. It is true that we might have come to a very different verdict twenty years ago; for while the democratic labour movement even then had achieved many substantial gains in defending the interests of the working class, those gains remained essentially partial and insecure until the development of the techniques of control over the processes of a market economy which are usually linked with the name of the late Lord Keynes, but which were also independently worked out by the Swedish Social Democratic government after 1932 and, for radically different purposes, by the Nazi government in Germany. The use of these techniques by the Socialist majority governments of Sweden, Norway and Britain, and in a less consistent manner by the New Deal administration in the United States, has furnished definite practical proof that the level of employment and the general direction of growth of advanced industrial economies can be controlled by democratic means in such a way as to abolish the dreaded trade cycle of traditional capitalism, and has marked the decisive change from the piecemeal alleviation of capitalist evils to the total transformation of capitalist society.

Parallel with this transformation, relations between the advanced industrial nations of the west and the underdeveloped countries have also been transformed—partly because of the growth of colonial and nationalist revolts against 'imperialism' both in its political and economic aspects, but partly also because of the growing impact of democratic opinion in general, and of socialist forces in particular, on the policy of the western governments. The two decisive events in this field were, of course, on one side the granting of independence to India, Pakistan, Burma and Ceylon by the British Labour Government, which marked an epoch and set a pattern, and on the other the development of various forms:of 'foreign aid' for underdeveloped countries (United Nations Technical Assistance, Colombo Plan, American Point Four Aid) which do not depend on private capitalist investment and are not directed according to the investor's profit-expectations, but according to the development needs of the underdeveloped countries as seen by the governments of these countries. Today, imperialist exploitation and the conflicts due to it are by no means liquidated, but the process of liquidation is far advanced. Parallel with the last violent conflicts in one group of cases, new forms of co-operation between former colonisers and former colonies are evolving in others. Moreover, the evident decline of imperialism has not led to permanent depression and deepening economic crises in the advanced countries, but has been accompanied by steady economic expansion there.

Nor has the decline of imperialism produced the intensification of rivalry among the imperialist powers predicted by communist theory. That picture was true so long as the advanced industrial countries were helpless in the grip of the economic cycle. It can rightly be said that the horrors of German fascism, as well as the military dictatorship in Japan, derived directly from the miseries of the world crisis of 1929–32, and to that extent the second World War was due to the exacerbation of great power conflicts by the failure of uncontrolled monopoly capitalism. Yet since the defeat of these anti-democratic régimes, co-operation among the western democracies has proved far stronger than their inevitable economic rivalry—thanks partly to the overwhelming economic preponderance of the United States, which no other western state could seriously hope to challenge, and partly to the new techniques of controlled internal economic stabilisation which facilitated the creation of corresponding techniques of international economic co-operation. The decisive milestone in this field was the Marshall Plan. Many other forms of economic co-operation must still be regarded as experimental and some of them are likely to fail, but the general trend can be expected to persist because it is—and to

the extent to which it is—founded on the structural transformation in progress *within* the western democracies.

An attempt to take note of these changes within the non-
communist world—the adoption of planning techniques for the
purpose of maintaining full employment, the advances of the
labour movements, the replacement of colonialism by the granting of self-government and independence, the development of
state-controlled forms of foreign aid—and to revise communist
theory accordingly was made in the early post-war years by the
well-known Soviet theorist of Hungarian origin, Professor
Eugen Varga; but Varga was forced by the upholders of orthodox Leninist doctrine to recant his heresy, and has not revived it
even since Stalin's death. Only the independent Yugoslav communists have come to recognise the growth of 'state-capitalist
and socialist elements' in the western democracies, and to draw
the conclusion that socialism may be victorious by other means
than that of communist dictatorship—that in advanced industrial countries it may be achieved by the methods of the western
democratic labour movement, while in underdeveloped countries with a weak bourgeoisie a socialist policy may be initiated
by non-Marxist, national-revolutionary parties or groups.

It is all the more important to realise that the formula of 'different roads to socialism', to which the Soviet leaders subscribed
in their Belgrade declaration with Tito in June 1955, and which
they elaborated at the Twentieth Congress of the CPSU, implies no similar toleration of 'reformist' roads on their part.
According to the congress documents, 'socialism' can only be
achieved by the 'dictatorship of the proletariat led by its communist vanguard', i.e. by a Communist Party dictatorship; the
difference between 'peaceful' and 'violent' roads to socialism
which is now admitted amounts to no more than the difference
between establishing such a party dictatorship by prolonged
civil war, as in China and Yugoslavia, or by a 'revolution from
above' using established parliamentary institutions, as in Czecho-
slovakia and other East European countries. But the fact, and
even the possibility, of socialist transformations of society
achieved by non-dictatorial means is still rigidly denied by Soviet doctrine as a 'reformist fraud'. It follows that the Soviet
leaders continue to regard *all* countries not governed by Com-

munist Party dictatorships as subject to the laws of capitalist decline; and this applies to India under Nehru no less than it did to Britain under a Labour government—regardless of their *tactical* interest in establishing friendly relations with such régimes for a limited period.

If the description of the Soviet bloc as the 'camp of socialism' and of the non-communist world as the 'camp of imperialism' are both wrong, then the analysis of the conflict between them as a clash between monopoly capitalists defending their privileges and the world movement of the working class is obviously equally false. The foreign policy of the Soviet Union is no more determined by working class interests than is, say, the distribution of income or the planned share of consumer goods production inside it; nor has western resistance to Soviet expansion been inspired primarily by capitalist interests, or even been backed by them at all consistently. Yet conflict there is, and conflict there has been under the most varying governments in the west, and under different generations of leaders in the Kremlin. What, then, is its character?

The answer is to be found in the nature of totalitarian dictatorship which can only justify its existence by the need to struggle eternally against an omnipresent enemy. As the dictatorship dominates all spheres of life, politics and economics, culture and religion, sport and family, as it extends its tentacles all over the world through the Communist Parties, so it pictures the infinite variety of social forces which offer resistance to its policies, both inside and outside its sphere of power, as so many manifestations of a single hostile force, the class enemy. To Karl Marx, capitalism was a historical form of economic and social organisation, subject to all the laws of historical variation and change; to the Soviet Communist régime of today, capitalism is a spectre of personified evil, unconsciously created in the image of its own totalitarian will to power—in the same way as the Nazi belief in the secret world rule of the Elders of Zion was unconsciously fed by the image of the limitless designs of totalitarian Nazism. The world is divided into two camps because Soviet communism is a totalitarian movement and régime, and because totalitarianism can only live by dividing the world into two camps— that of its tools and that of its enemies who must be destroyed.

None of the changes that has happened in the Soviet Union since the death and the subsequent dethronement of Stalin are intended to alter the fundamental character of the régime. Stalin is today blamed for having raised himself, with the help of the secret police, above the party—not for having perpetuated the dictatorship of the party itself long after its original revolutionary task had been fulfilled. The promised end of the horrors of arbitrary police rule, the transformation of the labour slaves into forced 'free' settlers are meant to make Soviet society more efficient as well as more tolerable; they are not meant to weaken the political monopoly of the ruling party, which is on the contrary to be strengthened by every means in the power of the present rulers. Their intention may, of course, miscarry; the weakening of authority by the destruction of the Stalin myth may force them to make further and unplanned concessions, until the party dictatorship itself dissolves under the pressure of the new social forces. Such a development, whether we judge it likely or not, would end the problem with which this essay is concerned; without the party dictatorship, Russia would be a great power like any other—with common or conflicting interests with individual other powers, but without the basic 'ideological' conflict I have tried to analyse. But while the party dictatorship lasts, the conflict will last.

The struggle, then, is not between a 'socialist camp' controlled by the workers and an 'imperialist camp' controlled by the capitalists. It is between, on the one side, a bloc of totalitarian states, controlled by party discipline from a single centre, in which every free labour movement or democratic socialist party, like every other form of democratic organisation, is outlawed; and, on the other, our own multifarious and ever-changing society which is not controlled from a single centre, which contains colonisers, colonies and ex-colonies, modern democracies and backward dictatorships, and advanced capitalist countries in various stages of transition towards a socialist form of organisation.

This struggle admits no neutrality in the fundamental political and ideological sense, however many states may have good reasons to remain technically neutral in the military sense, because totalitarian states and parties ultimately regard as their enemy any force not subject to their discipline. That ultimate hostility does not, of course, prevent them from seeking to divide their enemies and temporarily to secure the co-operation of one group against the other, both diplomatically and within the free countries. But such tactical co-operation, say with Colonel Nasser's régime against the west or with a 'popular front' coalition against a right wing government, makes as little difference to their basic attitude toward their temporary partners as did their wartime alliance with the western powers against Hitler.

Hence democratic socialist movements like our own are committed to the 'anti-communist' camp not as a matter of choice, but by their very nature; they exist only within that camp, their chances of achieving their aims are confined within its frontiers, and their refusal to submit to communist discipline makes them *ipso facto* the targets of unremitting Soviet hostility. As Mr. Khrushchev said, in answer to a question about the future ideological relations of social-democracy and communism put by Mr. Sam Watson when the Labour Party delegation to China passed through Moscow: 'In this field, there can be no co-existence'.

From time to time, the Soviet Communist leaders make an effort to blur this stark fact by suggesting co-operation between the communist and social-democratic parties for common immediate objectives, 'without regard to their theoretical differences'. Yet such 'United Front' proposals, whether put forward on the national or on the international plane, do not modify in the least the fundamental hostility of the communists to all democratic movements, since they are not based on recognition of the validity of democratic socialist ideas—not even of their validity for advanced democratic countries, as admitted by the Yugoslav Communists—but merely on a tactical desire to win democratic socialist support for some immediate purpose regardless of the fundamental rejection of these ideas. For that reason, communists have always followed Lenin's precept of supporting social-democrats in such 'United Fronts' just 'as the rope supports the hanged man'; and their treatment of the socialist parties of Eastern Europe, who after varying periods of coalition government were first infiltrated by police methods and finally liquidated by compulsory fusion with the communists has furnished a striking illustration for the meaning of this metaphor. Yet that procedure has once again been hailed as exemplary at the Twentieth Congress of the Soviet Communist Party—at the very moment when an effort was being made to inaugurate another period of 'United Front' manoeuvres. Nor could it be otherwise; for the admission of the permanent right of alternative parties to exist is clearly incompatible with the basic aims of a totalitarian world movement.

III

THE one incontestably true statement, then, in the communist doctrine of co-existence would seem to be that the conflict is irreconcilable—irreconcilable, that is, as long as the totalitarian party régime lasts in the Soviet Union. It can only end either with the nightmare of communist world domination, or with a decisive change within the Soviet Union, which would not, of course, reverse the results of state-managed industrialisation, but would put a stop to the all-pervading rule of the party and its revolutionary dynamism. But it is also true that irreconcilable conflict of this type does not exclude the prolonged co-existence of the two hostile worlds; in fact, conflict and co-existence are two aspects of one and the same relationship between them. For we agree with Mr. Khrushchev that irreconcilable conflict does *not* mean inevitable world war.

We have seen that the communist theory of the forces making for an ultimate clash between the two worlds is wrong— that the non-communist world is not dominated by desperate capitalist ogres ready to start a nuclear holocaust in order to save their bank accounts. But neither is it true, as certain western anti-communists have thought, that the communist urge for world domination must sooner or later find expression in some atomic Pearl Harbour, some ideological *Blitzkrieg* for the world stakes. That view is not based on a study of the actual method and rhythm of communist expansion, but on a superficial analogy with the experience of Nazi expansion; and while the two totalitarian systems of our time have indeed a number of structural features in common, there are also vital differences between them—differences which explain why Nazism has gone under in an orgy of destruction while Soviet communism has survived for almost forty years.

Nazism, being based on a doctrine of racial superiority, was self-limited in its appeal and could ultimately rely for its expansion on military conquest only. Soviet communism is universalist, addressing its message to all mankind and relying on the revolutionary forces produced by the 'contradictions of imperialism' to ensure its triumph everywhere; hence military conquest is only one among its methods of expansion. Nazism, consciously aiming at world domination by a small, nationally defined minority, could only hope to win by greater preparedness and a rapid succession of surprise attacks before its opponents had time to rally; reckless gambling was its only possible strategy. Soviet communism is convinced that the forces of history are on its side and that its strength must steadily increase at the expense of its opponents—hence it can afford to bide its time, to avoid needless risks, to wait for favourable opportunities and even to order 'temporary retreats'.

This is not to say that military conquest, including cases of unprovoked aggression, has played no role in the history of Soviet communism. As early as 1921, the Georgian democratic republic, constituted under a socialist government in accordance with the right of secession from Russia as proclaimed by Lenin, was annexed by an act of unprovoked aggression; and the Polish war of the previous year, started by a Polish attack on Soviet territory, had been deliberately turned, after the repulse of this attack and a Polish offer of peace, into an ultimately unsuccessful Bolshevik war of conquest aimed at revolutionising Poland. A similar attempt at conquering Finland for a Soviet communist puppet government was made under the protection of the Stalin-Hitler pact in the winter of 1939–40, and the Baltic states were annexed in the following year. I have already mentioned how, after Hitler's defeat in the second world war, the Soviet communist system was forcibly imposed on a number of east and central European countries which were overrun by the Russian armies, how it was also forced on North Korea, and how a similar attempt in Persian Azerbaijan was only abandoned under the pressure of the western powers.

But expansion by military conquest, though apparently the

method favoured by Stalin as most reliable in the interest of continued centralisation of power, has not been the only nor even the most important one; the victory of the Chinese revolution after a prolonged civil war and without direct intervention of Russian military force has been of greater historical impact than all the above-mentioned cases together, and Yugoslavia and Viet Nam have furnished examples of the same type on a smaller scale. Nor has communist expansion by either method been at all continuous; it has taken place in a few widely separated waves, dependent on situations when the world was shaken by great 'inter-imperialist' wars or their aftermath, and when deep conflicts among the non-communist powers offered Russia opportunities to embark on military conquest with very small risk. In the one case where the Soviet Union was involved in a great war—after 1941—she had certainly done her utmost to keep it away from her borders by appeasing the Nazi aggressor; in the one case where she encouraged open aggression without the cover of a favourable opportunity—the case of Korea—she evidently acted from a miscalculation, believing South Korea would not be defended by any major power, and even so was careful to intervene only by proxy and to limit the scale of the risk. The record shows that even before the advent of the H-bomb, the Soviet Union, while willing to use all seemingly safe opportunities for local aggression, at no time deliberately risked world war.

This is a fact of the utmost importance for the future of mankind. For it means that in the conflict between our evolving free society and Soviet totalitarianism we are not faced with the bleak alternative of submission or atomic world war—that we have a chance to survive without becoming slaves and to defend our freedom without committing collective suicide. The certainty that peaceful co-existence with the Soviet bloc is compatible with resistance to totalitarian expansion must form the starting point of any realistic doctrine of co-existence for democrats and socialists.

The means of such resistance must obviously depend to a large extent on the means used by the communists at any given time. In a period of open communist aggression or military threats, the principal—though never the only—means of resistance will inevitably have to be military. In future, as in the past, we must be prepared to repel local aggression by adequate military force as we did in Korea, and to answer the threat of aggression by measures of military preparedness, such as the arming of threatened borderline countries and the creation of a network of military alliances and bases. But in periods when the communist powers recognise that the chances of forcible expansion have become too small to justify the risk, and when they consequently seek to reduce the burden of their own military effort by putting the main emphasis of their diplomacy on 'peaceful co-existence', while concentrating their energies on domestic tasks, the opponents of totalitarianism must equally seek to reduce the military burden so as to gain increased freedom of political movement and to free resources for economic development. In considering any measure of disarmament or military disengagement, the continued basic hostility of the communist bloc and the possibility of a later return to agressiveness have, of course, to be borne in mind; hence the need arises for preserving a long-term balance of power and for continually developing new weapons. At a time of transition from a phase of communist expansion to a period of reduced military tension, such as we have lately been passing through, one obvious danger is that of premature slackening of vigilance.

But there is also the opposite danger of clinging to an out-dated order of priorities in fighting an enemy who has changed his methods of attack—of losing, for instance, political friends by insisting on the extension of military alliances in regions whose people feel no threat of communist aggression. In such periods and places, support for the modernisation of 'uncommitted' national forces, combined with explicit or implied guarantees and the maintenance of a mobile striking force for implementing them, may well prove both less costly and politically more effective than insistence on alliances which lack popular backing in the nations concerned.

The more acute the military threat and the more urgent the task of defensive preparedness, the more the specific role of democratic socialists within the free society tends to be submerged in the common effort to preserve their common freedom. Conversely, the less acute the specific military danger and the more the communists themselves put the emphasis on 'peaceful co-existence' in the intervals between their waves of forcible expansion, the more the defence of freedom against totalitarianism comes to depend primarily on political development *within* the great free communities—on their ability to solve their own internal and international problems in such a way as to deny the totalitarian enemy new political opportunities for expansion. It is here that democratic socialist movements, as champions of social advance within the free society, have their most distinctive contribution to make. Given a threatening emergency, any courageous democrat, however conservative, may rally the people of a free country to a policy of containment; but it takes a policy of constructive progress to avoid the repetition of the emergency by the successful practice of competitive co-existence.

IV

SUCH a policy of constructive progress may be considered under three main headings, corresponding to the three main 'contradictions of imperialism' on which the communists count—a policy of economic and social advance within the leading industrial countries, a policy of promoting self-government and independence for colonial territories and of fostering economic development in underdeveloped areas, whether still colonial or not, and a policy of promoting international co-operation within the 'free world' generally. To regard these policies merely as weapons of competition against communism is, of course, to look at them from far too narrow an angle; they are necessary in themselves to cope with the problems of growth of a free society, and would be as necessary if the alternative was not totalitarian revolution, but simply stagnation and misery. The point I wish to emphasise here is that, while in periods of acute military tension there may from time to time be conflict between the needs of constructive political progress and the needs of short-run physical defence (at least in the sense of a conflict about priorities), in periods of 'competitive co-existence' the needs of progress coincide with the most important needs of protection against communism.

The record of communist aggression is sufficient to refute the fallacy that constructive progress within the free societies would by itself be sufficient safeguard against the military threat from outside, once great totalitarian powers have been constituted. But this must not be allowed to obscure the truth that both in its origin and in many individual acts of expansion, totalitarianism has fed on the failures of development within the free world. German Nazism would never have come to power if German democracy had in good time found the means to overcome the scourge of mass unemployment; the Soviet conquest of eastern Europe would not have been possible if timely western rearmament and a policy of collective firmness had either prevented or decisively shortened Hitler's war; northern Viet Nam might not be communist today if France in Indo-China had taken British policy in India for her model.

Today a repetition of failure to solve the internal problems of advanced industrial countries is less likely; moreover Soviet communism, unlike fascism, is by its origin better adapted to profit from the unsolved problems of underdeveloped rather than of highly-industrial countries. It can be no accident that there have been successful communist revolutions in Russia, Yugoslavia, China and north Viet Nam, but never in any modern industrial nation; and a great deal of the attraction of communism in Asia and the Middle East today is due precisely to the fact that it presents itself as a method for achieving speedy industrial development by revolutionary means, combined with a rejection of the traditional dependence on the western 'colonisers' and even of their cultural influence. That factor, of course, links up with the sympathy gained by the communist powers in uncommitted Asia by their genuine and unequivocal rejection of any colour bar, as well as by their hypocritical but ostentatious anti-colonialism—hypocritical in that they themselves are oppressing and exploiting underdeveloped nationalities within their own frontiers, where they do not become visible as 'colonies'.

The outcome of the vital struggle for the future of the uncommitted regions of the world, which are largely the same as its underdeveloped regions, will thus depend on the ability of the leading western democracies to achieve a clear policy in three respects. First, they must realise that their principal interest is not to tie the underveloped nations to their side, which in many cases cannot be done without arousing anti-colonial resentments, but simply to help to ensure their independent development along non-totalitarian lines. Second, they must unambiguously dissociate themselves from the attempts of less enlightened western countries, and of reactionary groups within their own countries, to cling to concepts of racial superiority and to outdated forms of colonial rule, so as to reap the full benefit of their own progressive policies in these matters and to overcome the legacy of the past. And third, they must help the non-communist leaders of underdeveloped nations in devising and carrying out an economic programme for 'catching up' which can truly compete with the communist one—a programme which would have to be no less effective but would require fewer sacrifices from the masses, and could therefore be implemented by non-totalitarian means.

The rivalry in this last vital field is not simply a competition in generosity ('which side will give more aid'), nor even in generosity plus propaganda ('which side can offer the same amount of aid in more spectacular forms'). It turns above all on the impact of different *methods* of aid which are linked to different roads of economic development—in a manner clearly perceived by the Soviet leaders but not yet at all well understood by the west.

Most of the underdeveloped countries suffer from two kinds of obstacles to economic and social advance. One is the dead weight of traditional institutions and customs, linked with the interests of pre-capitalist privileged groups and often protected by religion, which obstruct modernisation—such as the seclusion of women among Moslem peoples, or the caste system and other taboos of Hindu society. The other is the basic poverty of the bulk of the people, which makes it extremely difficult to finance from private savings the amount of investment needed to improve the existing standards of living. These factors combine their effects when the rapid growth of population, partly due to traditional attitudes hostile to birth control, aggravates the poverty and increases the need for investment even to maintain the present standard. The first obstacle can be overcome only by a government supported by a popular movement animated by revolutionary faith; the second requires primary reliance on massive *public* investment. Communism offers both.

It follows that any alternative to communism conceived in either liberal or traditional authoritarian terms is bound to fail in the underdeveloped countries—that successful rivals to communism in these countries must themselves be movements of a revolutionary type prepared to build up their industry largely under state management. That is why the Indian Congress has lately pronounced itself, on Mr. Nehru's urging, for a 'socialist' programme—meaning primarily a programme of state-planned investment—and why Burma's successful resistance to years of communist guerilla warfare has been accomplished by a government based on the revolutionary Anti-Fascist People's Freedom League, whose core is the Socialist Party. In such countries, Soviet strategy is now based on the expectation that these movements cannot achieve their objectives without themselves becoming totalitarian—that they must either come to adopt the Russo-Chinese way under the pressure of their economic problems, or must fail and give way to their own local communists.

In fact, the outcome will largely depend on the rate of investment adopted, and on the role played by foreign aid in the process. If total investment remains insufficient to produce visible progress, economic stagnation will spell political failure and ultimately communist victory. If the targets adopted are excessive in relation to the total resources available, including foreign aid, implementation of the plan will require totalitarian measures which non-totalitarian governments cannot carry out. The problem for the opponents of communism is to devise programmes big enough to permit a steady improvement in the standard of living, however slow at first, parallel to efforts for long-term development, and to finance them without resort to communist methods of 'primitive accumulation'. That is possible only if the planners can be assured of substantial amounts of foreign aid for a long period ahead.

The danger is therefore not that the communist powers will outbid the advanced free countries in the total amount of foreign aid. They cannot dispose of the amounts required at a time when they are having to face the tremendous internal problems of Chinese development, and even if they could provide sufficient amounts, it would not be in their interest to do so—though it obviously is in their interest to supply enough to make a propaganda impression. The dangers are, first, that the total amount of aid available from *all* sources will prove insufficient for a non-totalitarian development, and second, that the communist aid will be given with the deliberate intention of involving these countries in one-sided long-term dependency, and in a way which makes the immediate raising of the standard of living, and hence the preservation of democracy, more difficult. The communist 'aid offers' are, in fact, investments of the type Hitler used for his pre-war penetration of the Balkans—arms or investment goods are sold in return for long-term bulk purchase contracts of agricultural produce and raw materials. If the west wants to preserve the international independence and internal freedom of these countries, it must offer them food as well as investment goods; it must not allow the Soviet bloc to provide the only markets for their agricultural exports; and it must meet the communist challenge by planning its aid on a long-term basis and not relying on forms of private investment based on the acquisition of property rights.

The difficulty of competitive co-existence in the underdeveloped countries is not how to offer *more* than the communists; it is how to see that the total amount of aid *from all sources* is sufficient for healthy development, and how to offer our share on realistic terms suitable for the long-term development needs of those countries. That requires not only the overcoming of the western taxpayer's reluctance to make the necessary sacrifices, but also of the constitutional obstacles to long-term aid programmes and of the traditional prejudice in favour of private over public investment. To that extent, the victory of the opponents of totalitarianism in the struggle for the future of the underdeveloped countries depends on the victory within the west, and above all in the United States, of progressive forces free from traditional capitalist blinkers. It also requires an understanding by the peoples of the advanced democracies, and especially by organised labour, that we may have to postpone an otherwise possible rise in our own consumption for the sake of poorer nations. In the period of competitive co-existence, sacrifice for foreign aid may prove as much a necessary price of freedom as a sacrifice for armaments did in a period of threatening war. But, while this is difficult, it is no more inherently impossible than was the victory of similar ideas first in the Lend-Lease programme and then in the Marshall Plan, or the post-war effort of Labour Britain to support a starving Europe and also to develop her own colonies even at a time of severe domestic austerity.

Finally, there is the problem of maintaining and developing international co-operation among the free countries—of preserving and extending the political unity of the core of the non-communist world in a period when it is no longer ensured by an acute military threat from outside. Thanks to the progress in the internal economic management of the advanced countries, the danger to this unity in recent years has come less from economic rivalry than from unsolved nationality problems, as in Trieste, Cyprus or the Saar, or from differences in the degree of insight shown in dealing with the independence movements of colonial peoples. But while this primarily suggests the need for stronger political machinery to deal with such disputes, there is need for greater coordination of economic policies based on common principles as well, if the achievement of full employment within the national framework of most advanced countries is not to be exposed sooner or later to uncontrolled disturbances of international trade.

The obstacle to such greater political and economic coordination, even among nations with common democratic traditions and common advanced economic and cultural levels and with an obvious desire to translate their common outlook into common policy, is, of course, national sovereignty; and the failure to date of all efforts to create federal institutions even among a small number of like-minded European nations seems to offer little hope of overcoming that obstacle in the near future. But it may well be argued that the plans for a political six-power community on the continent of Europe failed in part because their sponsors tried to create a closer form of federal union than was necessary for the practical tasks in hand, and in part—which is the reverse side of the same mistake—because they concentrated on a narrower group of states than is relevant to the most important problems.

Experience suggests that the really relevant group is the Atlantic Community, including the United States, Canada and Britain along with the countries of continental western and northern Europe, and that the form of co-ordination to be aimed at is that of a confederacy rather than a federation—the creation, that is, of permanent common political and economic organs of government delegates, tied to the unanimity rule but under strong pressure of public opinion to achieve agreement, and empowered to bind their respective governments once they do agree. There are still great obstacles to be overcome before that much can be achieved, and the results are bound to be extremely imperfect even if it is; but at least a confederacy of that type no longer appears utopian. It looks, indeed, as if a reform of NATO along these lines may be the next stage of progress in the international field, and the one on which realistic efforts should be concentrated.

V

So far we have considered the problem of co-existence with Soviet communism from the strictly defensive angle of 'containment'—how to prevent its expansion by either military force or by political victories due to failures within our free society. But must we take it for granted that while we have to engage in this unending vigil to prevent free countries from being lost, any nation once under communist control will stay enslaved forever? Is there no hope of 'liberation' for the unwilling victims of sovietisation in eastern and central Europe, no prospect of an abatement of the totalitarian dynamic in Russia itself? Is there nothing our policy can contribute to end the menace and burden of this conflict, even in the very long run?

Obviously, we cannot contemplate any idea of liberation by force or threat of force. Quite apart from the horrors of world war in the nuclear age, no democratic government would deliberately start even a local war by seizing a favourable opportunity and gambling on it; that is a technique in which we cannot compete with the totalitarians. Being unable and unwilling to act in this manner, the western powers could only harm themselves by threatening to do so—they would fail to impress their opponents and would divide their own peoples.

But renunciation of the aggressive use of force or the threat of force does not imply acceptance of the status quo of the conquests of Soviet communism. To the communists, 'peaceful co-existence' spells continuation of their war against the non-communist world by non-military means; and the democratic opponents of communism do not lack their own political weapons for exploiting in their turn the 'internal contradictions' of totalitarian communism. Of course it is in the nature of a totalitarian régime with its immense concentration of power that it may maintain itself even in critical conditions and against the opposition of a large majority of the people; the survival of the Stalinist régime in Russia during the famine and mass deportations that followed the forced collectivisation of 1929–31 is a striking example. But there is no eternal law that guarantees even such a régime against a combination of a severe internal crisis with political pressure skilfully applied from outside.

The first element of weakness in the Soviet bloc is the continuing resistance of large strata of the populations of the European satellite nations against an alien régime—a resistance that became visible in such actions as the Czech mass strikes and the East German rising of June 1953, in the mass departures of peasants from the Hungarian collective farms in the following winter, and in the Poznan revolt of June 1956; but also in the eagerness with which even the communist intelligentsia of Poland and some of the other satellite countries seized the chance of greater freedom of criticism, granted after the Twentieth Congress of the Soviet Communist Party, to try and make life more tolerable at home and also to increase personal and cultural contacts with the west.

Any uncensored influx of ideas from non-communist countries which penetrates the 'iron curtain' of the communist monopoly of information must inevitably strengthen this deep-seated opposition to Russian-imposed totalitarianism. So far, the ordinary workers and peasants in the satellite countries could only be reached by western radio stations, whose information and advice has often helped them to defend their interests without exposing themselves to reprisals, and to co-ordinate their action by learning of concessions already granted to their colleagues in neighbouring countries. Such propaganda must be recognised as a 'normal' part of co-existence with communism just as is communist propaganda in the free world—provided, of course, that it does not encourage acts of sabotage and violence.

At the same time, any chance for non-propagandist individual and cultural contacts—tourism, exchange of books and films, etc.—that is now arising should be welcomed as a contribution to the lowering of the ideological barriers imposed by the one-party state. Visits by western labour representatives and delegations, if undertaken officially, have a different character; they are political actions liable to be exploited propagandistically to discourage the democratic socialist opponents of the totalitarian régimes, and should only be undertaken after careful preparation and for clearly defined political purposes.

Yet encouragement of any form of resistance behind the iron curtain makes political sense only if the western powers are prepared to follow it up by diplomatic action in case of a real crisis. Its one conceivable aim must be to make the Soviet rulers reconsider whether the holding down of these unwilling populations is really worth the trouble; hence if a crisis breaks out, the moment must be used to press the Soviet government to set free the people concerned, and to offer negotiations on terms which might facilitate such a decision. For instance, it cannot be expected that even in a crisis the Russians would consider such a political retreat if it meant that the abandoned territory would be joined to the NATO area: even in a favourable situation, 'liberation by negotiation' will require agreement to leave the freed nation militarily neutral under international guarantee—in the case of Eastern Germany, it would require agreement on the armed neutrality of a united non-communist Germany. In a phase of reduced military tension, the political gain would be well worth the military loss. The fact that at the Berlin and Geneva conferences the Russians have shown no interest in such a deal—which was not proposed by the western powers either —cannot be considered as proof that they might not have been pushed into it in a critical situation, a few months after Stalin's death, if the west had taken the initiative to exploit it. Whether the chance was small or large, it was missed; but its example may suffice to illustrate the point that opportunities of this kind may arise again, and could be used to better advantage by western governments with a dynamic concept of co-existence.

The prototype of a second element of weakness is the conflict in which Yugoslavia broke away from the Soviet fold in 1948. The possibility of conflicts of national interest exists among non-satellite communist states—states based on their own 'national' revolutions—no less than among 'bourgeois' states; this could only be denied by Stalin by postulating that no communist revolution was possible anywhere without the guidance, the aid and indeed the physical presence of the Soviet Union, and that any government that refused to submit to Soviet leadership automatically ceased to be communist. Since then, Stalin's heirs have had to admit both the existence of independent communist revolutions and the independence of their leaders, and must seek to rely merely on the fraternal solidarity of all 'Marxist-Leninist' parties. Such solidarity is unlikely to survive any really severe conflicts of interest, and western diplomacy has in principle as much of a chance to work upon such conflicts within the communist camp as has Soviet diplomacy within the western camp. This is not to make a facile claim that Russia and China 'must' clash—evidently they have many major interests in common—but only to say that there are also potential conflicts between them, and that these conflicts *may* one day break the unity of the Soviet bloc, given skilful operation of western diplomacy.

Recent signs of a relaxation of Soviet control in some of the East European satellite states, and of the growing popularity enjoyed there by 'national' Communist leaders like Gomulka in Poland or Imre Nagy in Hungary, have caused some western Socialists to argue that we should aim at fostering in these countries a 'Titoist' development towards independence under a Communist régime rather than oppose that régime itself in the name of democracy. This view overlooks the fact that the Communists have remained small minorities in all these countries, and would have little chance of surviving without Russian backing; for this reason, the new Soviet leaders remain unwilling to grant them the same measure of independence which they have had to concede to the home-grown Communist régimes of China and Yugoslavia. If at present some of the 'national' Communist leaders enjoy the status of a semi-legal opposition, the people will certainly support them against the representatives of the 'Stalinist' policy of complete subordination to Soviet interests, and so should we; but like the people of these countries themselves, we should regard any steps towards greater internal freedom and national independence *within* these régimes merely as stepping stones towards their eventual complete self-liberation from the rule of the Communist minority. In particular, we must beware of the fallacy which equates any idea of overthrowing that dictatorship with the bogey of a return to 'capitalism' or the pre-war rule of the landowners.

The breaking up of the former big estates and the creation of new state industries in some of the more backward countries of Eastern Europe are irreversible social facts; the one-party state and its attempts at collectivizing the peasants are not.

A third element of potential crisis, demonstrated by the experience of Russian forced collectivisation mentioned above, applies also to countries which have undergone a 'home-grown' communist revolution. It arises from the attempt to force the pace of industrialisation of an underdeveloped country at all cost, and to finance the 'primitive accumulation' required for this by ruthless exploitation of the peasant majority. This attempt leads regularly to the introduction of forced deliveries of agricultural produce at fixed prices, and peasant resistance against that measure has to be broken by forced collectivisation, imposed as a means of political control far more quickly than would be rational as a means of increasing production, even in the communists' own view. At present this whole chain of causation is being repeated in communist China, with a serious risk that the consequences in loss of life and production may become even more terrible than they were in Russia. Nor is the achievement of a high level of industrialisation necessarily the end of crises of this kind. The position of the Soviet collective peasants, much improved in recent years by a series of concessions on delivery prices, may be placed in jeopardy again by new efforts, announced immediately after the Twentieth Party Congress, to reduce their remaining private plots and to turn them into a kind of wage-labourers working on piece-rates. The inherent inefficiency of the *kolkhoz* system, due both to the weakness of individual incentives and to the lack of a firm basis for calculating labour costs, is bound to produce ever-new experiments and social conflicts.

Finally, there is yet another 'contradiction' inherent in the basic mechanism of the communist 'permanent revolution from above'. It is that communist, state-managed industrialisation creates a large, privileged bureaucratic class, which, like every privileged class in history, has an interest and a desire to consolidate its position and to enjoy the fruits of office in peace and personal security; while at the same time the party régime can only justify itself by permanent either external or internal revolution, and thus can only live by keeping everybody, including the members of the new upper class, insecure and preventing them from settling down. Stalin's ingenious solution for that contradiction consisted in forcing the new bureaucracy to join the party, from which most of the old-style revolutionaries had been eliminated in the Great Purge of the thirties, thus preventing it from constituting itself as a separate group *beside* the party; but the conflict between the two inherent tendencies continues, even if all the leaders can be said to be both 'bureaucrats' and 'party men', and reappears from time to time in conflicts between leading personalities and their cliques. Fundamentally, the tendency of the party machine must be to keep the process of the permanent revolution going indefinitely, while the bureaucracy, including the professional military men, must wish to terminate it in the interest both of the upper class and of the people at large.

The problem has come to the surface in the criticism of Stalin voiced officially after the Twentieth Party Congress. The most fundamental criticism was directed against Stalin's doctrine that the class struggle must get more intense as 'socialist construction' proceeds, which was correctly described as a justification for the discovery and subsequent annihilation of ever new 'hostile classes' and for an unending prospect of persecution and terror. This suggests that the present party leaders find it necessary to repudiate the policy of the 'permanent revolution from above' and to offer peace and security to the new bureaucratic elites in an effort to preserve the primacy of the party after Stalin's death. But such a policy, if honestly carried out, must lead to a decisive weakening of the party because it would deprive it at least of its domestic *raison d'être*, and to a corresponding growth of 'Thermidorian' tendencies. Obviously, there is bound to be resistance to such a development and further conflict; and a clear-sighted western policy may help to influence the outcome by refusing prestige concessions to the ideologues, while seeking to meet the 'bureaucratic' leaders where the genuine security interests of the Russian state are concerned.

A democratic strategy of co-existence, then, like the communist strategy of co-existence it is supposed to answer, has three main aspects. Each needs a policy of military preparedness—though the communists can use opportunities for local aggression if they arise, while their democratic opponents cannot. Each needs a policy for exploiting the inner conflicts and weaknesses in the opposing camp—though here again the communists can be more unscrupulous in using force to overthrow hostile régimes, and far more brutal in suppressing opposition within their own territory. And each needs a policy for the internal development of its own system.

But it is in the different type of internal development that the fundamental contrast of the two worlds comes out most clearly. The internal development of the communist world—what we have called the 'permanent revolution from above'—aims at re-modelling society forcibly according to a preconceived pattern by an unending series of upheavals, tending allegedly to the final goal of a classless and stateless society, but in fact to an ever more complete concentration of all political, economic and even spiritual power at the summit of a dictatorial state. The internal growth of a free society is manifold and flexible, inspired by the abiding ideas of freedom and social justice, but seeking ever new concrete solutions in adjustment to changing conditions. That is why I believe that, despite the technical advantages of totalitarian ruthlessness, the free society is potentially superior to its formidable opponent in this long-term contest. But only potentially; only as long as we succeed in not only seeking, but finding ever new concrete solutions. Time was when the penalty of failure to advance was merely stagnation and delay. Today the penalty of such failure is a total loss of freedom. In the struggle for co-existence with totalitarianism, a free society must progress or perish.

II

THE POLITICAL ECONOMY OF
THE COLD WAR

THOMAS BALOGH

THE impact of economics on foreign policy can be viewed from two different angles. One can regard foreign policy as something dictated by power political considerations only (which, of course, include economic motives). Viewing it from this vantage point, we would consider what economic policies are needed to enable a country to carry a political decision into effect. Or, starting at the opposite pole, the economic position of the country may be taken as given, and the enquiry restricted to what foreign policy is compatible with it.

In the past few years a good many arguments have been conducted from one or other of these two basic attitudes. As they moved on entirely different planes, the clash between them could not yield fruitful results. What seems to be required is an attempt at an analysis which accepts an intimate interaction between political aims and economic policies without prejudging the relationship between the two.

Democracies are under constraint from the social implications of increased economic effort, which set effective limits to foreign policy. These barriers can be lifted only at times of great peril, and only at the cost of setting in motion forces of popular feeling which might prove uncontrollable. Nothing shows this more clearly than the history of the last years. Even at the height of the North Korean war, which was taken to indicate the imminence of other possible communist probings for weak points in the democratic defence, no effort was made to take even elementary civil defence precautions against an atomic attack though then they might still have been effective. No democratic government was then willing to enforce a full war economy, despite their own alarmist statements, and there could be little doubt that the extent and character of rearmament was severely circumscribed by the political impossibility of imposing drastic burdens.*

In the present essay, therefore, we shall keep in mind these limitations on policy, inseparable from the democratic process, while enquiring into the ways in which the threat to the existence of the western world, implicit in the existence of the Soviet, can be met. We shall, first of all, investigate the impact of the thermo-nuclear weapons on the economics of war and cold war; secondly, we shall enquire into the character of the Soviet challenge with due regard to the thermo-nuclear threat; in the third place, we shall analyse the relations of the members of the Atlantic Alliance to one another to determine what policy is the best feasible in the circumstances. Finally, we shall try to outline the consequences of our findings on policy decisions for the British Labour Party.

II

PREPARATIONS for the next war are usually impeded by the mistaken application of the experiences in the last. In the first World War the military deadlock in the west led to a decision which seemed due to economic attrition causing a breakdown at home. Consequently it was assumed that in any future conflict it would be economic staying power that would decide the issue. The policy of accumulating stocks of weapons was discredited.

The campaigns of 1940 and 1941 demonstrated the folly of this view. An overwhelming stock of accumulated offensive weapons, and the superiority of offence over defence, all but resulted in a German victory over a combination of countries far superior in economic potential. That potential, for want of time for its mobilisation, remained sterile. Only when the shock of the *Blitz* had been absorbed by Russian distances and climate

---

*The lack of preparation also indicated a certain disbelief in Soviet military aggression. America went further than Britain. But this effort entailed the creation of a psychological atmosphere which was nothing short of warlike, and which, in the following period, not merely impeded diplomacy, but did serious injury to those institutions of freedom which are the particular achievement and pride of the American revolution.

could the basic economic potential reassert itself. This seeming repetition of history confirmed earlier judgments. And in the first years of the Cold War economic potential was once more considered as the final arbiter in any armed trial of strength.

The successful explosion of a hydrogen bomb by Russia created a new position. In the first place the relationship of current economic potential to a stock of ready weapons once more changed. Long-run economic productive capacity has lost its meaning for total war. The offensive has once more gained the upper hand; economic potential will have been annihilated before it could ever be mobilised. Moreover, this terrifying capacity for destruction is embodied in relatively cheap bombs, even though the means of delivery still remain expensive. A comparison of productive capacities, beyond a certain minimum required to produce bombs and the planes or guided missiles to deliver them (and, of course, that minimum is still very considerable), is no longer meaningful. In a hydrogen war the only things that count are accumulated stocks and bases from which to launch them.

In the second place, however, the chances of annihilation have been equalised. The enormous advantage of large geographical size has been reduced, as the area of annihilation has explosively expanded. As the peril has increased so has the equality of the risk-facing countries. The advantages of large continents, which might well have been willing to endure ordinary atom bombs, has shrivelled. From the point of view of this island, by far the most vulnerable of the greater powers, this might not be a disadvantage. The change in the geographic chances of survival has profoundly influenced the relationship of the powers in the west to one another, strengthening our influence.

By equalising the chance of annihilation, however, the bomb has changed the basic relationship of countries and blocs to one another. The restraint shown by both parties in the three acute crises in the Far East, despite the strain on American emotions, has made it perfectly clear that total wars, because they mean total annihilation, have become impossible. The idea of deterrence rather than defence has come to dominate military philosophy.

True enough, this discovery also represents a nuclear

stalemate. The deterrent cannot be used without the certainty
of annihilation. Hence this stalemate does not eliminate the risk
of 'small' wars. This is the factor that prevents the pursuit to its
conclusion of the new shape of military thinking in our defence
planning. It is also the factor behind the maintenance of conventional forces, though the attitude of the west in general, and of
Britain in particular to disarmament seems to have become
utterly illogical since Russia has taken the initiative in proposing
the limitation of conventional fighting forces most heavily bur-
dening Britain. Moreover the dissipation of essential food-stocks
in this country shows that neither nuclear nor limited warfare is
expected. What is still not fully realised or admitted is that the
nuclear stalemate does not exhaust its impact by re-creating the
value of limited conventional fighting forces. The struggle for
men's minds and hopes, for their allegiance in the wide marginal
(and in the main uncommitted) areas of the world, becomes
paramount. Thus, perhaps somewhat paradoxically, the bomb
which destroyed the importance of economic factors as a means
of waging war, has not merely enhanced them, but endowed
them with entirely novel significance, as a means of maintaining
peace. It is in the field of economic and even more of social progress, and most probably in the two giant areas of underdeveloped Asia, that the struggle between the two economic systems
will be fought out.

No doubt a communist victory at the polls caused by a failure
of the west and the Soviet's more bountiful economic promise
could be resisted by force. But by the use of such force the west
would forfeit its great moral appeal and might also lose the very
values for which it first took up the cudgels. It is not sufficient
merely to win. We must try to win without losing ourselves.
Our superior endowments, material as well as moral, should
enable us to achieve our ends even while gladly accepting restraints on our means.

III

DOMINANT western thought—especially in official circles—has
conceived the Soviet threat almost exclusively in military terms.
Accordingly the main effort to meet it has been in the field of
military preparations and defence treaties. Close co-operation

has been achieved on that plane, but has tended to exhaust itself there. Consequently the opportunity created by the relaxation of tension, and the decrease in the arms burden, could not be used for intensified efforts at buttressing the weakest points in the socio-economic fabric of the western world, or of those marginal areas in which the Soviet challenge can be expected to be most potent.

This view of the nature of the Soviet challenge is not difficult to explain. The nonconformist Protestant tradition, which noticeably pervades all orthodox liberal thinking, strains against a detached appraisal of Soviet economic developments. While professing idealism, its adherents tend to conceive of the success of a social and economic system almost exclusively in material terms. A system which is despotic and cruel cannot be conceded to be efficient. Any attempt at a detached analysis of the Russian position immediately calls forth the uninhibited vituperation of the critics of the Soviet, eager to demonstrate the failure of the Soviet by its inability to provide an increased standard of life.

This argument, even if it were true (and, apart from certain foodstuffs and housing, it certainly is not), would be beside the point. An increase in living standards was not the immediate aim of Soviet policy. What the Soviets have only too well succeeded in achieving in the last twenty-five years is to create a powerful industrial machine which can be flexibly used for whatever purpose they choose. The Soviets were able to accomplish this by mobilising a largely peasant population and providing it, by forced abstention from current consumption, with an immense accumulation of capital equipment. The startling success of the Russian war effort showed eloquently how misleading was the ex-communist and extreme *laisser faire* view of the capacity of the Russian productive system, even before the war.* At its height, Russian munition production was almost

---

*According to an American appraisal the relative magnitude of the major belligerents' munition production in 1944 was roughly as follows: United States 100; Germany about 40; USSR over 35; United Kingdom about 35; Japan about 15; Canada less than 5. *The Power of Victory: Munitions Outlook in the World War*, R. W. Goldsmith. *Military Affairs*, Vol. X, No. 1, Spring 1946, p. 71. On recent developments see Soviet Economic Growth (ed. Professor Bergson) and the ECE Economic Survey of Europe in 1955.

50 per cent higher than the British. What perhaps is even more interesting and significant, Soviet productivity in munition production proved remarkably high, hardly inferior to either that in Britain or Germany. Here there was surely food for thought for our military economic planners.

Methods have been developed to correct Soviet statistics of production for over-statements in measuring output which are inevitable in a period of violent change. Even a conservative appraisal of the evidence available seems to indicate that after the ravages of the war the Soviet were able to achieve a very rapid recovery: from a level barely two-thirds of pre-war to which they had been reduced in 1945-6, by 1950 the pre-war levels were probably surpassed. The rise in output might have been at times as high as 20 per cent per annum. Since then the rate of expansion has necessarily decreased. From restoring a battered productive system in which, even despite the destruction, much basic fixed investment was preserved, the Soviet progressed to break new ground, a more laborious task.

Nevertheless, it seems probable that the increase in total Russian national output remains at least of the order of magnitude of 6 per cent per annum. It might well be higher, possibly as high as 9 to 10 per cent. The rate of growth in manufacturing production alone seems to have been substantially higher—as high as 11 to 12 per cent, possibly even more. In other words Russian manufacturing production would double every seven years or so and total national income every twelve years or less.

This compares with an increase in American manufacturing capacity of roughly 5 to 6 per cent per annum since the war and with an increase in Britain (apart from the drop in 1952-53) of about the same order of magnitude. Overall production in the west has increased much less, between 3 and 4 per cent only. Germany alone in the west has achieved an intensity of investment, and consequently a rate of expansion, which is roughly of the same order of magnitude as, and might at times have even been slightly higher than, that of the Soviet. It should be noted that this western record contrasts remarkably favourably with the pre-war performance of individualist countries. It has, moreover, been associated with an inflationary tension which most orthodox economists and governments are visibly unwilling to tolerate, and which they can hardly permit in the absence of direct controls, which have now been abolished even in Britain.

Soviet output per head, which in 1928 was a mere fraction of that even of the poorest western country, has undergone a startling change. It appears that in steel and engineering Russian productivity is approaching that of Britain. With overall productivity increasing at a rate which seems thrice that in most western countries, Russian output per head will soon surpass that in the most highly developed countries in western Europe and begin approaching that of America.* As the population of the Soviet Union and its satellites in Europe is roughly that of the western European countries, this means that Russia will enjoy a vast absolute preponderance of industrial power.

Nor is there any reason for complacency about the future. There is no reason why the Soviet Union should not be able to sustain this menacing rate of expansion. Admittedly they are no longer helped by the existence of productive capacity which merely needs repair. It is also certain that they have exhausted their most fertile lands and most obvious natural resources. It is also true that they cannot count on the same unlimited reservoir of manpower which they have hitherto been able to tap.

But against these unfavourable factors there are important offsetting influences. In the first place, with increasing national income per head, they will find it increasingly easy to expand investment without imposing sacrifice on the consumer. The recent reduction of armaments is a further favourable influence. Secondly, since the capital equipment actually in use in the Soviet Union is much younger than that in the western countries, the rate of physical depreciation is less. Thus a greater proportion of gross investment represents a true expansion of manufacturing capacity. This fact is now very familiar even in western countries with a lower rate of growth. In the third place, with increasing national income economies due to large scale production increase—though in Russia, where the introduction of new methods and new products is a political decision—this may not

*The implications of a higher rate of increase in productivity still seem to be imperfectly understood. A difference of only 3 per cent per annum would compensate for a 100 per cent initial disadvantage in some 24 years.

be as important as in countries where production in most cases starts on a small scale.

Finally, the Russians might feel secure enough to supply their needs beyond certain basic levels (corresponding to a wartime minimum) by foreign trade. According to reliable reports, food prices are about twice as high in terms of manufactures as in the west. Thus on the basis of the most orthodox comparative cost principle an exchange by Russia of goods in which she is relatively more productive against those in which she is less so would be beneficial. She could, therefore, outbid the west in the search for food and raw material supplies without any 'sacrifice'. There can be no doubt that the Russian decision to concentrate on industrialisation has paid off in a most startling manner. As the production of manufactures in the Soviet Union seems to increase three or four times (or even more) faster than agriculture, the Russians could well afford to assume very onerous terms of trade even without any wish to embarrass the west by economic warfare.* †

Nor is this all. Though Russian consumption has been increasing at a lower rate than national income, its absolute rate of increase since 1947 has been high, and was further accelerated in the so-called Malenkov period. This does not mean, however, that investment in heavy industry (i.e. industry producing

---

*Russia could easily have used her powerful gold reserves to buy meat when Britain was at loggerheads with the Argentine or to obtain oil from Persia and ship it in her own tankers. But beyond such occasional interventions foreign trade retains permanent advantages for her, and it is interesting that even now this remains unexploited. Instead, there are offers of loans and technical aid which, though politically embarrassing, are economically far less dangerous. Soviet economic strategy remains rather ill-advised.

†The control of strategic materials by the west was justified in the short run; it must have had a disruptive immediate effect. The longer (2–5 years) effects, however, must have been disadvantageous to the west; the Soviet Union was forced to fall back on itself and make itself independent of basic foreign supplies. This was accomplished in the end without any visible diminution of the rate of increase in total production. Moreover, trade within the Soviet bloc, and internal rationalization and standardization of production, were necessarily and artificially fostered. This must have been especially true in China which would more naturally have gravitated to trade with the west. The rigidity of Allied economic policy thus served in the end to stimulate Soviet development. cf. Postscript, page 77.

producers' goods) has been reduced absolutely in favour of investment in houses or consumer goods. What happened was that the rate of its increase was reduced. But for reasons we have discussed this does not mean that the rate of increase of total national income and of living standards will necessarily decline. If this analysis is correct Russian supplies of consumer goods will, in the foreseeable future, surpass even some of the more advanced countries in the west, such as France, though not reaching the levels of the richest for a considerable time. Actual living standards will be lower; quality comparisons seem to be still decisively against Russia, and the west enjoys a great advantage in a vast fund of accumulated durable consumption capital —houses, household goods, etc.—which is not reflected in figures of current output. The psychological impact of this fact is bound to be momentous.

Developments in China are equally worth considering. Capital investment there has apparently risen to 8 per cent of national income in 1954, and was to attain over 12 per cent in the following year. In view of the relief experienced as a result of the end of the wars in Korea and Indo-China, and the intensification of Russian help, these figures are not implausible. Nevertheless, they represent a tremendous achievement. The liquidation of the richer classes, the ruthless land-reform and the tremendous pressure exercised on all to limit their consumption, all this was needed to carry it out. They undoubtedly aroused bitter, if ineffective, hostility and thus weakened the hold of the régime. They nevertheless meant that a transformation of China has begun at a rate far quicker than would be possible (without a much greater amount of foreign help) even in a relatively less poor underdeveloped area under a democratic régime.

One thing more needs to be noted. There is very probably some truth in the complaints of the relatively richer Soviet satellite countries in Eastern Europe and the more prosperous areas in Russia itself, such as the Ukraine, that they have been systematically 'looted'. This 'tribute' was used to promote economic development in the poorest and remotest areas of Asia under Communist domination, which enables an overall growth far in excess of what could otherwise be maintained. Soviet planning, especially in the peripheral areas, has been guilty of gross blunders and waste apart from being pitiless and cruel. But the elimination of vested interests, the capacity of being able ruthlessly to disregard age-old customs, unquestionably frees great energies for reconstruction and permits the mobilisation of effort which elsewhere is impeded by these customs.

Nor are all the economic achievements of the Soviet system due to its totalitarian character. The Gosplan, it appears, first works out several schemes for the general directives on which all subsequent detailed planning will be based. An extremely flexible system has been brought into being. Once the heavy industrial sector and investment plans have been elaborated, any difficulty in respect of any one consumer industry can be dealt with either by changing the turnover tax or the factory price or both. Thus wage changes (at any rate since the currency reform —before that there was a sharp inflation) represent decisions to change *relative* wages for reasons of equity or economic need such as trying to influence the supply of labour. *General* increases in productivity, which in capitalist countries, at any rate in prosperous times, find their expression mainly in rises in wages, seem in the Soviet system to be reflected in reduction in prices. Wages, moreover, can be planned to give maximum incentive. Thus a slight inflationary tension, in the sense of demand exceeding supply at quoted prices, is maintained not by increasing demand but by the reductions in price. The great advantage of the system is that managerial talent can be almost entirely focussed on the technique of production, and we know from our own experience how progress is speeded up when recurrent marketing problems do not occupy almost the whole of the energy of the higher managerial staff.

Its success is a sufficient proof of the effectiveness of a combination of partial planning with a slight inflationary tension. The absence of individual ownership makes possible a ruthless rationalisation of production, as well as the speedy introduction and generalisation of new techniques. Considerations of private profit as against social advantage do not hold up modernization. Production and productivity are stimulated by careful attention to competitive emulation and due honours to the successful. New products can be introduced at once with the full economies of large scale production without having to wait for the development of mass-markets and the elimination of competitors. The inflationary tension no doubt produces shortages of goods in the Soviet Union, but it cannot result in cumulative price movements due to speculation. Nor will these windfall profits or capital gains lead inevitably to wage demands. Thus investment can be kept at a level far higher than can be attained in a system based on stimulating consumption and new needs, as the individualist system necessarily is. In this sense the Soviet has a basic advantage. But some of these conditions of faster progress could be reproduced in a mixed economy based on a democratic political system. And the large gap that still remains between Russian and western productive capacity leaves us still time to readjust western policy.

Thus we can conclude that, far from representing a complementary economic area from which Britain could obtain food and raw materials as in the past, the Soviet Union has become a formidable industrial competitor. No doubt in certain specialities, especially producers' goods, Britain could conduct a profitable trade with the Soviet—probably being paid in gold. Russia also needs certain industrial raw materials (e.g. wool and rubber), and China is still in the first stages of her industrialisation and is thus still prepared to spare something of her scant food-supplies to obtain machinery at better terms than are now offered by Russia. Thus it would be wise to encourage as much trade with the east as possible in order to lessen its drive for self-sufficiency. But the old comfortable notion that east-west trade could be a substitute for an intensive development of our own supplies of primary commodities is a complete delusion which only fellow-travellers can swallow. We shall be able to export certain specialised manufactures (especially capital goods) in return for gold, and in the long run in return for other manufactures, but the basic character of east-west trade has changed for good. A completely new approach is needed in our policy-making.

To that problem we now have to turn.

IV

THESE realities, the threat of annihilation and the threat of being overhauled and surpassed by the Soviet, with all that this must in the long run entail economically and politically, are hard to face. The British observer, especially if he is a member of the Labour Party and a Fabian Socialist, is thrust into an emotional and intellectual situation which is awkward because its elements are contradictory.

Theoretically Britain could choose between a number of conceivable policies. But in actual fact the choice boils down to two alternatives: a complete renunciation of narrowly national or imperial (or rather Commonwealth) aspirations, an intimate mingling in a 'western' alliance with all the limitations on policy that implies; or the retention as far as possible of more intimate connections (especially in economic matters) with the Commonwealth, and possibly western Europe, in a somewhat less close association with the United States and Canada, while striving to secure for the narrower area the greatest possible independence and maximum strength. Alliance with America is implicit in both.

Ever since the end of the war there has been, quite naturally, a powerful urge towards the closest association with the U.S.A. and towards strengthening the Atlantic Alliance eventually to include a 'political' tie. This drive has had varied motives, and has been forcefully supported by ideological and material arguments. In particular it was identified by the leadership of the Labour Party with a true 'internationalist' solution.

The material arguments are clear. On the one hand it was obvious that Britain, or even western Europe, could no longer defend itself against a Russian attack. Even a minimum of preparations turned out to involve burdens which in fact could not be carried without substantial American help.

These were the factors which determined the attitude of Labour when in office. The Conservatives, the orthodox economists and the bureaucracy saw another important objective in this co-operation. They hoped that this policy would lead to Britain reverting to the pre-war economic system. Once currency convertibility was re-established the owning classes could once more hope to exercise a veto over the economic and social policies of any government. If this implication of the choice was at all clear to Labour—which is doubtful—it certainly did not weigh in the balance. A number of ingenious if not very convincing formulae were evolved both on the economic and the socio-political plane to justify this attitude. This meant that the American interpretation of the 'optimum' way to peace and prosperity through the 'free' price mechanism had to be accepted. No doubt the absolute rule of the price mechanism acting through free markets, the whole paraphernalia of *laisser faire*, were rather difficult to reconcile with conscious planning of the economic and social destinies of the nation to which Labour was pledged. But the U.S. was relentless in the defence of these principles, which as we shall see presently were much in her own short-run material interest, and Britain immediately after the war was in dire need of American help—having been brusquely deprived of Lend-Lease supplies before she had a chance of readjusting her economy. Thus even people of progressive views were driven to accept the American policy.

This acceptance of obvious contradictions was made much easier by several factors. In the first place physical controls over the economy—which was associated with wartime shortages and had never been reconsidered in the light of peacetime needs and possibilities—were extremely unpopular. In the second place, as a pathetic afterglow of Britain's century-old industrial supremacy, the hold of the Free Trade Dogma, however inapplicable it was to her post-war position and problems, remained unbroken.

Ten years are a sufficiently long period in which to assess the success of an economic policy. The lessons of the attempt to force the world back to the more or less unfettered play of the free price mechanism are—as in the 1920's—far from encouraging.

There was nothing wrong in the assumption that the mobilisation of American strength, if not essential to the solution of the problem of the non-Soviet orbit, would immeasurably speed it up. It proved astounding. Having sustained a productive effort during the war equal to that of all the other belligerents put together, it continued to expand after the war was over. Between 1949 and 1953, the U.S. succeeded in expanding arms expenditure from \$19.3 billion to \$51.4 billion. Far from experiencing any strain, private consumption and investment also expanded, the former from \$180.6 billion to \$230.6 billion, the latter from

$32.5 billion to $51.4 billion, or each the equivalent of a sizeable fraction of the total British national income. Nor is this a mere monetary mirage. American output capacity for steel, aluminium and chemicals expanded in five years by more than the total of British production of each in the corresponding period. There can be no doubt that the U.S.A. possesses at least three fifths, and possibly more, of the total investment capacity of the non-Soviet orbit. Per head this represents completely crushing superiority over the rest.

American rearmament, far from damaging the economy or thrusting it into bankruptcy, immensely strengthened it. Conversely the successful cut of armaments from $51.4 billion a year in 1953 to $40.8 billion in 1955 without a major crisis shows great advance in mastering the problems of economic management. It should not be forgotten, however, that arms expenditure is still three times that of 1948, and that demand was sustained by an exceptionally favourable conjuncture of circumstances including an exceptionally aggressive sales campaign calculated to increase luxury spending while capital investment was expanded to a record level. Investment even at this level seems still to be well within America's physical capacity, while elsewhere strenuous measures have to be applied to restrict a much smaller effort. Three fifths, if not more, of total investment both in manufacture and in agriculture is thus concentrated on a relatively small portion of the area and of the population of the western world. In this disproportion originate many of the economic difficulties and political weaknesses of the powers opposed to the Soviet. If nothing else, the accumulation of huge agricultural surpluses at a time when the underdeveloped areas have to cut their exiguous investment programmes for fear of inflation shows that the western world is far from having solved its economic or political problem. The vast profits —on the average 17 per cent per annum—on U.S. foreign investment clearly indicate that little can be expected from direct private investment (in contrast to low interest bearing loans and free grants) towards a solution of the problems of inequality or even of development. Practically the whole of the surplus produced by such investment accrues to the investor and not to the undeveloped area. Even more fatuous is the slogan 'trade not aid', as trade relaxations benefit the underdeveloped areas only by improving their terms of trade—to an altogether insufficient degree and far too slowly. As even this improvement rarely leads to increased investment (in contrast to grants) it can be dismissed as a way to counter the Soviet threat.

The theory behind the policy of liberalisation was, in the words of one of its most enlightened defenders* stated thus:

> In the absence of political unification the principal coordinating force available to the free world is the operation of unfettered markets for goods and capital. In the broadest sense therefore the defence of the free world and its institutions depends upon . . . the unrestricted operation of these market forces

in order to equalise

> the relative rates of economic growth in the free and Soviet areas of the world.

It was hoped that 'freeing' enterprise would result not merely in speeding up capital accumulation and the increase in productivity. It was also thought that it would decrease the gross inequality of opportunity between the rich and the poor. There was, of course, no historical justification for either of these hopes, which were based on logical fallacies. Even in highly developed and dynamic countries the whole array of the Welfare State, progressive taxation and careful regulation and subsidisation of agricultural production was needed to stem inequality from increasing. In international economic relations identical—but, of course, vastly stronger—forces encountered no obstacle.

After ten years the failure of the attempt is perfectly obvious: the attempt to 'liberalise' trade nationally and internationally

(i) has been unable nearly to match the Soviet rate of economic progress. Indeed outside the U.S. and Western Germany—both of which represent exceptional cases— the liberalisation of trade, by causing a worsening of the balance of payments, enforced a policy of dear money which is inimical to investment and so to an increase in productivity;

*Professor Mikesell, *Foreign Exchange since the War*, p. 523

   (ii) has worsened the distribution of incomes at home, and
has thus created social tensions which do not help an increase in investment as they lead to wage struggles;

  (iii) has also increased the inequality of income and wealth
between the countries of the non-Soviet orbit.

It is problematical whether total real production per head in
poorer areas outside the Soviet Union was any higher in 1950
than in 1913, though of course production figures in primitive
peasant countries are subject to grave doubt. Moreover, far
from abating, this tendency seemed to have been *accelerating as
a result of the second World War* until conscious measures of planning were adopted in important poor countries such as India
and Italy. Food production in most underdeveloped areas up to
1950 continued to lag behind the increase in population. The
increase of the world's food supplies was almost entirely concentrated on North America.

Surprisingly enough, much the same was true of the progress
in industrial output. Outside the Soviet orbit it has been almost
entirely concentrated in the *rich* areas. Industrial production outside the Soviet Union in 1952 was only four-fifths higher than
in 1938. In the U.S.—which represents all but one half of the
total—the advance is $1\frac{1}{2}$ times as great as total output in 1938,
and is about the same in the richest countries of the Commonwealth. In western Europe the advance is only 35 per cent, and
France managed to catch up with its 1929 output only in 1951.
*In the rest of the non-Soviet world the increase is only 10 per cent as
against an expansion of population of 20 per cent.*

It should be noted that this relative and absolute impoverish-
ment took place despite several exceptionally favourable factors.
There was first of all the large reduction, due to the wartime
inflations, of the real value of the debt owed by poor countries.
In many cases (as in the case of India and the Middle East) military expenditure by the creditor countries enabled these countries to repay their foreign debt altogether and in addition to
accumulate large reserves. These reserves were used to support
investment which in many cases was planned for a period ahead,
as in the Colombo Plan. Moreover, all these factors relieved
the constant pressure on the primary producers to sell their
goods; their terms of trade improved and thus their ability to

purchase foreign goods increased. What would have happened in the absence of this relatively favourable development is difficult to picture.

This story of failure would have been far starker had the precepts of those who wanted to rely on international trade to increase the national income and international equality been successful. The truculence of the Soviet and the outbreak of the cold war saved the intellectual and emotional situation in the western world in general, and in Britain in particular, in more senses than one.

The first attempt to liberalise trade occurred in 1947. Within a few days the American loan of $3,750 million, which was to have served for years of reconstruction, was exhausted and Britain was saddled with a vast problem of repaying a loan she could not utilise for productive reconstruction. Europe had to face the choice of either cutting income drastically and enduring mass unemployment or going back on the *laisser faire* principles of the U.S. loan agreement. The dilemma was solved by Russia brutally walking out of the Conference on European Economic Cooperation which had been hurriedly called to consider the breakdown of economic reconstruction in Europe.

The American Congress could therefore be persuaded to return to the principles of Lend-Lease and UNRRA. Despite the brilliant success of the conception underlying international redistribution according to the capacity to bear the burden, both these instruments had been brusquely smashed as a result of the propaganda of the liberal school, which wished (as in the 1920's) a quick return to 'normalcy'. Now once more large scale help was granted to the weaker areas. But the American Administration went further; it initiated common planning for western Europe and consented to the establishment with its help of a common payments system. Both represented a discrimination against American exports, and both could have been used to make Europe permanently more self-sufficient.

The recovery consequent to this change of policy was remarkable. Unfortunately the possibilities inherent in the new conception were not given full rein. Trade liberalisation once more prevailed and the machinery for common planning was left to decay. In consequence two more crises occurred at two-

yearly intervals. After each the U.S. relaxed its drive for con-
formity and Europe was permitted to recover. The second of
these crises occurred after the outbreak of the Korean war, when
the relative capacity to carry the burden was disregarded;
American aid to Britain, which had been suspended in 1950,
was reintroduced and buttressed by 'offshore' purchases (i.e.
deliberate placing of orders in Europe) and direct U.S. military
expenditure. Without this expenditure recovery in Europe in
the teeth of the American setback of 1953 would not have been
possible.

As these 'emergencies' passed pressure was immediately felt
to return to 'normalcy', to cut aid (mainly to help in balancing
the Budget) and to liberalise trade. Little effort was made, quite
comprehensibly, to liberalise American imports where this con-
flicted with the maintenance of employment, or to refrain from
controlling trade in agricultural products. Nor would a more
'liberal' policy have been an adequate answer to the pressing
problem of inequality in the western world. The improvement
in the terms of trade of the rest of the western world would
hardly have increased real income abroad sufficiently to raise
investment. Only direct aid to the poorer areas could accomplish that.*

These considerations necessarily lead to the conclusion that
the American attempt to impose a 'liberal' solution on Britain
and the western world has failed to create a stable position of
strength. Only in those poorer countries in which conscious
measures of economic planning for development were adopted,

---

*Nor is there any chance of private investment stepping into the breach.
The vast underveloped areas of the nineteenth century have been filled up.
There is no incentive for the private capitalist to invest in the poor areas;
unless expansion is consciously planned, the narrowness of existing markets
deter him. It is quite clear that American capital cannot and will not undertake the duty carried by Europe in the first decade of this century. In actual
fact U.S. private investment has hardly ever topped the billion dollar mark.
Yet its vast profitability, due to the superior capital strength and technical
knowledge, has doubled U.S. foreign assets since the war. As U.S. wealth
is so much larger than that of any other country a programme of full investment abroad would mean that the U.S. would cumulatively come to own a
large part of the *increase* of the capital equipment of the world and so increase
the share of absentee ownership, which would be politically intolerable.

e.g. India and Italy, has there been any notable progress since 1950 towards higher income per head. The situation of and outlook for Britain in particular have been worsened, despite generous measures of U.S. economic help, not merely relatively to the Soviet, but also the U.S. and Germany. Throughout the post-war period Britain was prevented by the continued liberalisation of foreign trade and decontrol at home from breaking out of the vicious circle of low investment, insufficient increase in productivity and high consumption demand. In 1947 and 1949, in 1951 and again in 1955 she was forced to adopt policies which cannot but slow down her progress even if the U.S. continues to prosper. Only the manifest maintenance of equity in income distribution could induce the trade unions in Britain (as against Germany) to adjust their claims to what would be manageable without causing international instability. But no conscious policy of high investment and equity of sacrifice could be evolved. In this failure the pressure of American economic concepts played a notable part.

This conclusion does not reflect either on the integrity, sincerity or on the capabilities of the American policy-makers. The two wars and their disruptive effect on the old-world economic system have faced the Americans with unprecedented problems. Indeed, had the Americans been able to provide a permanent solution to the problem, they would have to be hailed as having performed an almost superhuman task and adapted themselves in an unprecedently quick time not merely to the leadership of the world but also to the solution of problems which have never been tackled before, and which could be tackled only with the greatest difficulty within the social and intellectual framework in which we have been brought up.

A number of well-meaning and indubitably sincere authors have been at pains to tell us that the U.S. is no longer a bulwark of unregenerate capitalism, of *laisser faire*. And in well documented books, articles and broadcasts they submit to us proofs stretching from minimum wage legislation through social security to the celebrated high dams of the Columbia and Tennessee, to the federal power grids and to the elaborate protective system securing fair shares for the farmer. They point to the immense improvement of the distribution of income and the desperate need of any U.S. Administration, on pain of dismissal at the next election (and U.S. elections are always inexorably near) to maintain full employment, which means the bargaining power of the great trade unions. They conclude quite rightly that economic power is no longer unlimited, that the popular franchise has made a return to an old-fashioned disregard of the interests and opinion of the vast majority of the less privileged impossible. Democracy is too firmly entrenched for capitalism to disregard it.

All this is undoubtedly correct. The headlong flight of the Republican chieftains of the Treasury from dear money and the abandonment of efforts 'to put value into the dollar' in 1953 (in other words to bankrupt producers and lower wages) as soon as output showed the slightest downturn have adequately proved this view. The recurrence of a really devastating depression is unlikely. Unfortunately this is not enough. The weakness of the rest of the non-Soviet world is too great to be able to tolerate even a minor American depression if protracted. The tragedy of the Western World is that the discrepancy between the U.S. and the rest of the world has increased so much, so fast, that even the progress in social consciousness in the U.S. cannot safe-guard the prospects of the rest of the world.

Moreover the enlightened policy of the State Department and the Economic Co-operation Administration, has been the direct consequence of the Soviet menace, and not, as some would say, the fear of a slump, or pure humanitarianism (though that has played a larger part than some of the 'tough realists' in England would think). Indeed, the Truman doctrine and aid to Turkey and Greece, as well as Marshall Aid, were elaborated in 1947 when the attention of the American public was riveted on the further possibility of serious inflation. The more traditional attitude of the American Administration to international economic problems, the attitude which tried to make the world safe for American exports, would hardly have been overcome without it. Indeed, even the Russian threat was insufficient to modify the stand of the Treasury and of the American domi-nated International Monetary Fund in 1949, against the more hopeful experiments in unifying Europe. This was repeated in 1951 after the Korean war thrust the western world into renewed crisis, and more recently in 1955–6 after the relief given in 1952–3 by the U.S. to her allies.

Thus it was not revival of a New or Fair Deal attitude, but the fear of further communist military victories, and mistaken Russian tactics, which ultimately brought about the change in American external economic policy. Only if we understand the American scene shall we be able to influence it towards a continuous broadening of present policies of international cooperation in the sense of planned development of poorer areas which the Labour movement had accepted as a necessity. It is, of course, possible that with the passing of time, and if the war remains cold, measures which have been accepted only as an emergency might be retained as the permanent expedients of international social and economic cooperation in the non-Soviet world. But we should not close our eyes to the fact that the measure of acceptance these policies have already gained was due to a state of fear of Russia, of an intensity which is difficult to explain and which has its own dangers.

However that may be, it is clear that even if it were in the interest of Britain to accept those ultra-liberal dogmas on international economic policy which have led to increased inequality and repeated crises, there is no reason to believe that the U.S. at this juncture would herself accept its logic and grant *unilateral* tariff concessions, or desist from using her superior lending power and other inducements to push exports. Nor is there any internal reason why she should do so. She is rich enough to be able to afford this 'depression' of her national income by 'less than perfect' use of resources. If this view of American reciprocity is justified, then British participation in a drive for trade liberalisation becomes absurd. This conclusion is strengthened when we reflect that the U.S., which in some sense would most 'benefit' from such liberalisation, repudiates it when it is applied to her own awkward problems.

So long as the truculence and aggressiveness of its policy isolated the Soviet, the NATO policy of concentrating on the military problem, of giving economic aid only in emergencies, did not lead to a fatal weakening of the coherence of the western world and of its hold on the 'neutral' belt. And if the atom bomb seemed to separate the fate of the continental U.S. from her European allies in case of war, the argument that America's nuclear monopoly was the only shield of the west, especially of the west of Europe, carried weight.

But Russian tactics have changed, even if not their end-strategy. Calculated isolationism has been abandoned by the Soviet. The marginal non-communist areas (and the breakaway Yugoslavia) are being wooed by words and by offers of material favours to come.

Thus the cold war, which ensured the emotional and intellectual solidarity of the west, has, if not ended, subtly changed into what is now generally known as 'competitive co-existence'. In this new situation, especially as it is coincident with (and to some extent due to) the maturing of Soviet economic progress, the re-examination of policies pursued since 1947 (or at least 1950) is in order. It was a feeling of emotional outrage against the Soviet Union which led to the acceptance of the burden of that policy. It is doubtful whether it would continue unimpaired even in Britain if Russia showed greater moderation. But even if she did such re-examination would still be needed. In large, marginal and therefore probably decisive, areas which are not committed to the west, western ideals—which seem safe in Britain and on their way to full re-establishment in the U.S. after a period of panic and doubt—mean little, if anything. To a vast majority of people in Asia, Africa or South America democracy did, and does, not exist, or has existed very nominally indeed. If anti-communism is to be based on a moral appeal policies which sufficed during the acute phase of the cold war will no longer do.

The task of the west would have been very much eased if the basic character of Anglo-American foreign policy had not been quite so exclusively based on regarding the Soviet Union as a purely military threat. For in that case the change in the approach to the problems of underdeveloped or marginal areas would not so clearly come as a result of Russian blandishments, but as a natural outcome of principles which have triumphed in the domestic social and economic scene in the west, and in their triumph destroyed the gloomy Marxist forecast of the inevitability of growing social tension, the opposite of what happened in international relations.

V

THE so-called 'internationalist' solution failed to buttress the non-Soviet orbit in general in the face of the communist challenge. It was an even greater failure in the solution of Britain's particular problems. It prevented a more imaginative and forward policy of economic planning in the British Sterling Area at a time when some deliberate sacrifice on the part of the metropolitan country might still have secured that feeling of loyalty, of common interest and adventure leading to the establishment of a third, well integrated and elastically coordinated economic system capable of meeting continental giants on equal terms. What in fact happened was an economic Balkanisation of the British Commonwealth in which even regional cooperation and specialisation (say in West Africa or in the erstwhile Asiatic colonies) soon might become impossible. The elevation of the Liberal idea of self-government into an absolute dogma, the concomitant, suicidal (and to some extent consequential) drive towards liberalisation which excludes all common economic planning and mutual help, has created a situation from which only the industry of the Dominant Economy of the U.S. can derive benefits, but from which the poor areas will find it increasingly difficult to extricate themselves.

The fear of American pressure, and the formidable Conservative class interest which hoped by this liberalisation to re-establish an undemocratic control of the propertied interests over the elected Government, do not fully account for this loss of opportunity under the Labour Government to make the most of the favourable situation which followed from the existence of wartime controls in the Sterling Area. It was due also to the unwillingness of the bureaucracy to pursue economic planning. This unwillingness was partly a consequence of the fear of responsibility, but mainly the result of the incapacity of the Civil Service as at present constituted and recruited to run a planned economy. And at no stage of its period in power was the Labour Government willing to reform the structure of the Civil Service, or even conscious of the need to do so. Thus the Free Trade Dogma, which was so profitable to Britain in her days of industrial supremacy but which had become detrimental to her national interests, received a further spell of dominance. It gave

a comfortable intellectual and moral basis for the policy of decontrol which all governments pursued, despite its fatal consequences for the national interest.

The resistance in the Labour Party to what might be called a
neo- or social-Imperial policy was intensified by the fear that
such a policy would not be very popular with Labour electors
precisely because it would entail burdens which could be shed
by the policy of encouraging 'self-determination'. (There is little
doubt that the growing 'liberalism' of the Conservative Government in colonial affairs is due to this reason.) The fact that an
'imperial' policy in this sense would mean not exploitation of
the colonial areas but a conscious redistribution of wealth and
income in their favour in order to create a cohesive system is
shirked. Hostility to new responsibilities, which are in fact inescapable for a Socialist, is politically better clothed in terms of
the well-worn phrases of anti-imperialism.

It should be recognised, however, that a policy of recreating
an effective economic unit between Russia and the U.S. would
represent a substantial burden to Britain, a burden which could
hardly be carried by the 'better-to-do' alone.

As a result of this post-war failure, the difficulties of Britain
pursuing an alternative policy are considerably increased. In pre-
war days of sterling convertibility, the Sterling Area was nothing more than a loose collection of countries which kept their
currencies stabilised on sterling because of the importance of
Britain as a market. The growth during the war of a closely knit
Sterling Area was a real (if completely unrecognised) gain for
Britain. Control over foreign payments (i.e. payments to countries outside the Area) prevented or at least slowed down nerv-
ous flights of capital. Capital movement from Britain into the
Sterling Area, however, remained free. This had momentous
consequences for foreign trade. London became the financial
clearing centre, and all transactions within the Sterling Area
were thus provided with automatic finance. Thus an important
preference was introduced for Sterling Area supplies, as other
supplies remained subject to severe control. The post-war reconstruction of Britain's foreign markets was potently aided by
this arrangement. On the other hand the Asiatic Dominions
were able to obtain unrequited imports against their wartime

accumulation of sterling balances. This represented an immeasurable boon at a time when distress in other Asiatic areas secured important victories for the Communists.

The Sterling Area was politically an anomaly; it did not contain the whole of the Commonwealth—Canada remained very decidedly outside. Some non-British countries on the contrary were members. It is partly this anomaly which has prevented effective and continuous consultation on policy between members, and has led to an irrational distribution of capital investment within the Area favouring the rich against the poor. Britain did not at any point try to organise the Sterling Area even as loosely as Europe was organised under Marshall Aid. Thus in its dealings with OEEC and America the British Government could never claim to represent a large and well coordinated economic area rich in natural resources and not merely a small island intent on snatching short-term advantages at all costs.

The recreation of an effectively functioning Sterling Area at this late stage would certainly not be easy. The political bonds with many colonies which remain members have been loosened. American influence has lately undermined the membership even of those of the colonies which might contribute most to the maintenance of a balanced triangular trade; the establishment of Central Banks has been recommended both for Malaya and Nigeria. While this need not necessarily mean a disruption of the existing bonds it can be (and is likely to be) used for that purpose.

No doubt each of the erstwhile members will in the end feel themselves menaced in one or the other of their export markets when they are no longer protected by the preferential arrangements implicit in the membership of the Sterling Area. Burma has experienced the consequence of U.S. dumping of rice, Australia that of wheat and fruit. But the attraction of cheap imports from the U.S. and of American grants and loans proved irresistible at first.

Thus any effort on the part of Britain to recreate an effective Sterling Area must imply the recognition of the need for large-scale aid to those territories. This aid might come in two main ways: long term bulk purchase agreements and assistance in capital investment. It is obvious that the colonies on their part

c

will have to recognise that such aid can only come if they grant preferential treatment to British exports, and do not impose a deflationary policy on Britain through calling for payment in dollars for supplies sold to Britain in order to be able to increase their imports from elsewhere.

The greater the instability and uncertainty about agricultural prices, and the more intractable the problem of American agricultural surpluses, the more attractive the guarantee of stability will appear to the dependent territories. The faster agricultural progress can be promoted in these areas, moreover, the greater the benefit for Britain. For the supply of these goods which we need will be increased (and their price decreased) while the demand for those products which we are able to produce will increase, thus enabling Britain to make fuller use of the economies of large scale production in certain specialised lines of manufacture without impeding industrialisation of the former colonies in others. The whole process is a beneficent and cumulative interaction strengthening the only bonds that will remain between the metropolitan country and its erstwhile dependencies when full political self-government is granted. By separating economic planning from the decentralisation of political decision-making, a democratic socialist basis might be found in Britain and her former dependencies to answer the challenge of the two giant continental economic systems which now threaten to overwhelm the weaker countries of the world. A closely co-ordinated system of economic planning might combine economic centralism with political liberty.

Such a policy could also serve in helping to pacify the Middle East, where excessive preoccupation with misconceived military considerations had led to an almost complete collapse of British influence and opened the door to communist infiltration. Yet as the Persian oil dispute clearly showed, there is no likelihood under present conditions of military intervention even to save so valuable an investment as Abadan. If, as seems inevitable, British and western European dependence on Middle-Eastern oil supplies increases irresistibly, a reconsideration of political intelligence and tactics in that area is acutely needed. Here again, we are confronted with the desperate consequences of Whiggish political policy combined with an even more Whiggish disdain for taking note of developments outside the charmed circle of those who are admitted to the Compound.

A programme of conscious promotion of economic development in the areas of predominant British interest, made coherent and interdependent by the resuscitation of the Sterling Area, would be burdensome to the centre. But unlike the present fetishist striving after the prestige of 'sterling looking the dollar in the face', of the 'status of sterling as an international currency', a prestige which inevitably results in weakness (not unwelcome to those who wish to use it to smash the strength of the trade unions), the sacrifice exacted under the alternative policy would restore the basis of British economic viability and independence. But it would certainly necessitate the availability of some £400 million rather than £300 million for foreign investment and grants in aid, and some further sacrifice in the shape of worsened terms of trade.

The monotonous recurrence of acute balance of payments crises in the post-war period has made it clear that the economy has been overburdened with demand on it, while decontrol has increased its vulnerability and decreased its power to concentrate on investment. Before any strengthening of our international bargaining and lending position can even be thought of, this fundamental weakness has to be remedied. Two alternative methods exist to deal with the problem. Either demand has to be cut down, or the rate of increase in production must be greatly increased. Up to a point it is possible to cut demand by selective controls and divert it away from imports without causing unemployment. But a recurrence of such excess cannot be dealt with in this manner without eventual detrimental consequences for the international competitive position of the country. There can be no doubt, however, that the policy of decontrol had ill effects on Britain's balance of international payments and standard of life. The loss of preference in western Europe and the Sterling Area implicit in exchange restrictions meant an automatic shrinkage of British export markets which was not offset by an increase in outlets in the U.S., while the liberalisation of imports from America (coincidental with the decline of the Sterling Area) added to the unbalance. All this powerfully contributed to the worsening of the terms of trade which in

1954–55 was once more the prelude to the crisis. The incapacity of British export industries (much aggravated by decontrol) to match American delivery dates was the final factor.

It is, of course, possible to regain 'flexibility' and cut back demand by disinflation through high rates of interest. But this way to flexibility is an expensive one. It must be purchased by pressure on investment, by slowing down expansion and by incurring all those unintended and harmful social and economic consequences—such as especially trade union resistance to technical progress and a general hesitation of investors to make commitments—which must be avoided if stable progress is to be secured.

There is, however, a perfectly safe way to salvation. It has been ever since the war fiercely resisted by all liberals, economists and civil servants. It is by increasing the rate of investment and thus of technical progress and productivity. The success of Germany and the Soviet Union, each in its way, in accelerating economic progress proves conclusively the feasibility of the policy. The resistance in Britain to the obvious solution of the national problem would be surprising indeed—all liberal economists of the nineteenth century concentrated their praise on the glories of thrift and investment—if we did not recall that under modern British political conditions a high level of savings would hardly be tolerable if it could only be achieved through an increased maldistribution of the national income, or through a shift of distribution towards profit as happened in Germany. It could, of course, be easily managed without such worsening if the increase in savings were in the form of collective savings, i.e. a Budget surplus. The resultant investment need by no means be collective or nationally owned. The savings could be pumped into the private sector either by repaying debt or by underwriting private security issues by Investment Boards specially constituted for the purpose. This incidentally would limit a further growth in the inequality of the distribution of property —an important consideration for a progressive government. The alternative would assuredly involve further wage claims and stifle the attempt in 'inflationary' balance of payments difficulties.

One obvious source of increasing grants and investment, especially abroad, is represented by the overblown military budget, which is in no relationship (even after the sharp cuts administered in 1952–3) with the capacity of Britain to bear her full burden relative to the U.S. The origin of our present weakness can be traced back to the conference of the so-called 'wise' men where the American experts seemed far more on the spot than the British representatives. According to Mr. Butler rearmament added £250 million a year to the deficit in the balance of payments, and if no agreement is arrived at on a German contribution to the maintenance of British troops there (which would indubitably have been easier before rather than after the grant of sovereignty to Germany) it will increase much further. Despite the cut in half of the original rearmament programme, the weight of the British contribution necessitated a sharp cut in both consumption and investment after 1951. In the U.S. both consumption and investment continued to expand during rearmament, reaching records all along the line in 1953. When expenditure was cut in 1954, this gave rise to a fall in national income which was made good only in 1955. These contrasts show that the net share of Britain in allied expenditure was far too high. The aid of £400 million for three years promised by the U.S. shrank away under the hostile gaze of Congress once Britain assented to her own contribution.* All in all the share of the total burden of the Alliance borne by Britain was and remains excessive. Military commitments are not easy to scale down. A determined effort will have to be made to do so to the tune of at least £300–400 million a year. Ways must be found, of course, to prevent the saving from being dissipated in increased consumption.

*This story is identical with the relative effort during and after the war. During the war U.S consumption increased in real terms by some 20 per cent, while British consumption was curtailed by approximately the same proportion. Moreover the conditions attached to Lend Lease impaired the country's long-term export capacity. After the war the British contribution —£1,300 million military expenditure, £600–£700 million in political aid and at least £1,000 million in lost export opportunities already prior to 1951 —amounted to some £800–£1,000 million *more* than the total grants and loans received—i.e. £2,100 million from the U.S. and Canada—even if we disregard the repayments and service payments already made to the U.S. on the post-war loan. This has not been recognized either in Britain or in the U.S.

It is in the increase in investment, therefore, that we must look for a solution of our problem. A speeding up of our economic expansion from say $2\frac{1}{2}$ to at least 4 per cent—still well below that even of Germany—would represent an annual increase of resources available of some £250 million a year and increasing at a compound rate. It is clear that any actual sacrifice of living standards—small as it would be if arms expenditure is pared down—need only be very temporary. Once the transition to a high investment economy has been accomplished all demands on the economy can be met with greater ease.

It is clear, however, that a mere increase in British investment capacity would not be sufficient to achieve the purpose. In the ten years since the war Britain has achieved a very creditable external capital surplus (apart from the loans and grants received which, as we have seen, did not represent a *net* benefit, but were merely channelled *through* Britain). All of this surplus, and an appreciable contribution from the dependent areas (especially West Africa and Malaya) in the shape of an increase in the debt of the Sterling Area as a whole to these—perhaps its poorest—members, went to finance the development of the richest areas of the Commonwealth, especially the Pacific Dominions and South Africa. In so far as a large part of this development was directly competitive with existing productive capacities in the U.K., it weakened the Area as a whole and decreased its overall viability. It should be added that the insufficiency of capital investment in Britain and the consequential inability to meet the Dominions' requirements in capital goods contributed to the desire to establish heavy manufacturing industries which in the longer run must prove a duplication of facilities. The lack of coherent planning in the Sterling Area, the lack even of a permanent Secretariat which could easily have been organised in the immediate post-war period, has earned bitter fruits. For this the Bank of England's relentless drive, shared by the Treasury, for empty financial prestige is mainly responsible. While the Pacific Dominions and India resolutely regulated their capital flows to the Sterling Area, no such control was exercised in London.

If a programme of deliberate development is to be undertaken in the Sterling Area in order to consolidate it and render

it more interdependent, such control will be essential. It must
be matched with control over investment in Britain. Control of
building and of the use of steel should be sufficient in this respect, especially if some measure of supervision over the export
quotas of the large concerns in the country is achieved possibly
by indirect means such as tax concessions. It is impossible in this
context even to hint at the changes in the administrative organisation and recruitment which such a policy would imply.

VI

THE drift in the affairs of the western alliance, the loss of the
atomic monopoly, the loss of China, the loss of Northern Viet
Nam, the growing unrest in colonial areas and the introduction
of police régimes it implies, the weakening of the western hold
over the Middle East, the increase in the international inequality
in income and, since 1954, the pressure on investment in the
weaker areas which presages its further accentuation; all these
cry out for a change in policy. There is no doubt that both the
relative material strength of the west and its moral impact are
being sapped by the present unimaginative and rigid approach.
A combination of verbal frightfulness and bluff and boast with
material incapacity to deal with the elementary social and economic problems of the alliance (and of the uncommitted areas)
does not presage victory. The increasing nervousness of the
west, the claims of success made without solid proof, are warning signs of failure.

It is this growing evidence of failure that might in the end
induce the difficult job of halting the drift. We have already
pointed to the two means by which the western alliance as such
and Britain in particular could achieve this end. Investment and
redistribution are the twin means of salvation, the need for
which has to be hammered insistently into minds whose common sense has been perverted by the unceasing flow of *laisser
faire* dogmatism subsidised by vested interests.

I readily admit that the proposed insurance against subversion,
revolution and disintegration might not work. Redistribution
through the flow of grants and loans on preferential terms on an
insufficient scale might increase and not allay discontent. The
development initiated might undermine established institutions

and restraints which have hitherto maintained stability, without giving sufficient hope for swift improvement to avoid a forceful overthrow of the existing social order. The way proposed is not without risk, but there is no hope whatever in any other alternative. We must question the wisdom of bolstering up small, weak and corrupt régimes in critical areas merely because they are anti-communist.

It should be noted that all organs needed for a reversal of policy exist. The periodic breakdown of liberalisation has successively thrown up administrative organs needed in the U.S. (whose ever-changing initials pander to political fashions—from Economic Co-operation to Mutual Aid—but which are fundamentally serving the same purpose under differing disguises), and has also created international organs such as OEEC. The institutions created in the heyday of universalistic liberal optimism—such as the International Monetary Fund and the Bank —can also be adapted to the new interventionist economic tasks.

Anyone with a modicum of common sense will readily admit that such a reversal of policy will not be possible without at least faint American acquiescence. And given the complete dominance of the U.S. within the non-Soviet orbit in the economic and technical field, such a reversal of policy will not be really effective if active American participation in the new venture cannot be secured.

It was, as we have seen, this very fact which was so influential in winning adherents to the policy whose ill-success we have been analysing. Could Britain flout America? Could she afford to pursue an independent, even contrary, policy? Would America not fall back towards isolationism, or alternatively, start upon a policy of retaliation which would bring Britain to her knees and in the process smash the western alliance?

The discussion of these problems in England is bedevilled by an ambivalence resulting from simultaneous feelings of envy and superiority, by the reaction against the only too sudden change of the status of England in relation to America. Individuals are accused of anti-Americanism who are far less critical of some features of U.S. policy than some Americans themselves. Indeed it is not easy to know exactly what is to count as 'American' in this context: is it the purblind anti-Communism

of MacCarthy or the enlightened analysis of Mr. Walter Lippman?

These suppressed emotions sometimes result in a panic but
baseless fear of American isolationism. But only those who really
attribute infinite stupidity to the American political system can
fear U.S. isolation in the sense of America retiring behind a fort-
ified moat in a huff in present circumstances. America became
isolationist, as Mr. Walter Lippman pointed out in his illumin-
ating essays on the basis of American foreign policy, because she
could afford to do so behind the shield of the British Navy.
Isolationism moreover was a moral issue for America and forms
in some way one of the most elevated moral principles in American conduct. But the present position has no resemblance to
that of the 1920's. Only two world forces remain. Thus it is
contradictory to argue at one and the same time that the Russian menace is overwhelming, and that there is an acute danger
of the U.S. leaving us in the lurch. The loss of Europe to the
Russians would be a serious, if not decisive, setback to the U.S.

For these reasons, British basic bargaining strength in relation
to America is far greater than generally thought. Nor does the
present fashionable view of the threat of American isolationism
merely imply that the Americans are quixotic if not stupid. It
also implies, unjustly, that they cannot be swayed by moral
considerations. Yet as the American attitude to colonialism in
general has shown, the view that American foreign policy is
activated entirely by selfish motives and power-opportunism,
is more untrue than in the case of most large countries.

The underestimate of the great force in the U.S. of moral
arguments, the underestimate of the even division of opinion
and thus the possibilities for determined moral leadership, these
are the explanation of much of the failure to obtain American
cooperation in a redevelopment of policy towards meeting the
Soviet economic threat in vulnerable areas. President Truman's
Fourth Point, the advice given in the Gray Report for increased
economic help, might easily have become official American
policy had they been reinforced by timely British pleas and
British leadership in sacrifice. No protest was ever made here
against the recent American thesis that private investment and
freer trade would solve the problems of the west.

It should be noted that a successful attack on inequality and poverty would embrace a gradual transformation of the present overblown and unbalanced military pacts of little intrinsic value into mutual economic development agreements, based not merely on trying to meet the insatiable needs of intrinsically unsound social structures by free grants which cannot achieve their purpose, but on the steady promotion of social reform in the recipient countries. This is essential, if for no other reason than that it seems impossible to demand contributions from the 'richer' countries to bolster up the wealth of rich exploiters who happen to live in undeveloped areas.

On the economic side an enlargement of the powers of the International Monetary Fund will be needed to transform it into an effective International Central Bank able to create credit in case of need. There should be a parallel transformation of the International Bank (now merely a limited Fund) into an International Development Authority whose funds should be provided by all 'high income' countries contributing an increasing proportion of the yearly increments of their national income. While no one can reasonably be expected to demand an *actual cut* in the standard of life of the contributors, there can be no political objection to *foregoing an increase* for the buttressing of the position of the west.

It would be difficult at this juncture to persuade the U.S. to contribute to organs in which the Soviet are represented—e.g. the proposed special fund of the U.N. (SUNFED). Their objections, the fear of being outwitted and their sacrifice used for Communist propaganda purposes, are rather misconceived, for the west would still be in control. Everybody knew where and how UNRRA obtained its supplies, and its activities unquestionably buttressed American influence. Moreover, there can be little doubt that non-committed areas would prefer a universal organisation for channelling economic aid. However, *ad hoc* agencies of a mutual character could easily be created—like the Colombo Plan Organisation for instance—to get over this difficulty.

The pattern for the planning of such programmes is fairly obvious. They must try to achieve a double aim: in the first place they must secure an increase in the productivity of fairly large coherent and interdependent areas; and, in the second place, and concurrently, social conditions will have to be raised by health, educational schemes and the finance of pre-industrial investment such as communications and public utilities (including electrification and irrigation schemes). The latter are the condition of a successful accomplishment of the former—but in the absence of foreign help would compete for the exiguous material resources available and thus prevent all progress.

The need to rationalise production over large areas, a need due to the increasing importance of mass-production methods, as exemplified in the vast advances made by the U.S. and the U.S.S.R., demands that preferential arrangements between potentially interdependent countries should be permitted. This might take the form of currency control, bulk purchase or preferential tariff concessions. All these have been outlawed at the insistence of the U.S., whose vast territory is an area of 100 per cent preference and which could make no or little gains in this way. The compulsory opening of each of the scores of small countries' markets on equal terms confers upon her an unfair advantage which stands in the way of equal progress.

Equally important means of progress would be arrangements —through buffer stocks and bulk purchase guarantees—to stabilise the price of primary products, the pressure upon which since 1954–5 has presented acute problems to the poorer areas of the western world.

A simple enumeration of these conditions of success is sufficient to show that, at best, a shift in policy will take a lot of time and a lot of doing. To persuade Congress to take the economic threat of the Soviet more seriously than the military or conspiratorial will be difficult. To induce them to throw the purpose of all orthodox liberals to the winds and return to the policies of the Marshall Aid period in economic, monetary and foreign trade matters will be more difficult.

It would be foolish to expect quick success. What is needed is that Britain should at last realise the terrible drift downwards in political and economic power, the unfavourable consequences not only to herself but to the whole world of the slipping of her force, and brace herself for a change in her disastrous economic, especially foreign economic, posture. British opinion is not as

yet united. The Anglo-American alliance must not be ruptured
by rash or violent moves. Steady British persuasion and relentless pressure towards the new policy will, in my opinion, gather
momentum. It will receive support in the U.S. itself, and in the
end victory will be achieved far more easily than now appears
conceivable, let alone probable.

British strength is needed not merely because it would enable
the pursuit of an enlightened policy of international redistribution of wealth and income, but also because her moderating
influence is weakened by dependence on the U.S. Military
strength thus borrowed in the end results in political weakness.
The 'reason why' of a forward policy of capital accumulation is
that it would enable us not merely to fulfil our moral obligations to poorer areas, but would restore our international balance, which has been sapped by doing too much on the basis of
too little. The fulfilment of our moral obligations and the safe-
guarding of our political influence would then no longer lead
to continuous embarrassment. Uninterrupted accumulation is
the sole way to cure the economic weakness, which at present
leaves Britain each year less able to intervene effectively.

Only through our own example and exertions can leadership
be given to a western Europe which has been drifting, and
whose drift might easily deteriorate into a collapse of the present NATO conception of the role of Germany. While the neutrality of Germany might under certain conditions represent a
major victory for the west (as it would if it followed from the
evacuation of the eastern zone), it might easily come about after
an actual rout of our present policies due to defection by the
west Germans.

Nor can we hope to influence the United States in any other
way. In the long run, and from the global point of view, this
last is perhaps Britain's most important task. There can be no
question that technical progress and capital accumulation have
enabled the U.S.A., if not to end poverty in the western world,
at least to assist in initiating a programme of international development sufficiently impressive to capture the allegiance of
the vast marginal territories in which the competitive struggle
of our time will be fought out—if indeed we escape annihilation.

POSTSCRIPT

This essay was written at the end of 1955. The obviously agonising reappraisal of American and NATO policies which manifested itself in the first half of 1956 in a spate of contradictory statements by the President, Mr. Dulles, Field-Marshal Montgomery and others, shows how faulty western intelligence was in assessing the character of the Soviet challenge. Having started from a position of overwhelming superiority in economic strength, the west has been reduced to a point where it must almost helplessly watch the attainment by the Soviet Union and its allies of equality in economic bargaining power if not in actual resources. The use of barter deals in arms by the Soviet Union in the Middle East was the first sign of the loss of western paramountcy. The growing volume and attractiveness of Soviet trade and aid offers are a further warning. Unfortunately the failure of Britain to give a moral and material lead in the directions discussed above (and forcefully put forward by Mr. Gaitskell on behalf of the Labour Party) has resulted in a *cut* of American aid by Congress at a juncture when the American political leadership was paralysed by the impending election. At home Britain succeeded in stopping economic progress altogether, as a result of trying to balance international payments by orthodox means. It has also ceased in the U.S.A. in spite of a record level of fixed investment in both countries. The obvious failure of NATO policy in Germany is a further consequence of missed opportunities. In all these directions Soviet gains are unmistakeable.

The unilateral Russian decision to demobilise a part of their conventional fighting services further highlights the urgency of the problem. Even if the greater part of the saving thus achieved were spent on atomic weapons, any further acceleration in Russia's development would spell not merely political discomfiture for the west in general, but would raise acute economic problems for Britain in particular. This *economic* threat would be aggravated if discontent in the Communist orbit lead them to import food and consumers' raw-materials against exports competitive with Britain.

III

BRITISH DEFENCE POLICY

JOHN STRACHEY

GREAT sympathy must be felt for the Chiefs of Staff, for the Defence Ministers, and for all those responsible for the planning of British defence policy in the nineteen fifties. For it is probable that never before have the basic factors with which they must reckon been in so rapid a process of transition.

It is not always recognised, moreover, that these rapidly changing factors are of two kinds, technical and functional. To take the technical factors first, most people are aware that the technique of warfare appears to be in a state of 'permanent revolution'. No sooner has one extraordinary development taken place than it is overtaken by another. Nuclear fission is overshadowed by nuclear fusion. The Mach 1 jet bomber is no sooner evolved than it is threatened with obsolescence. Looking a little further ahead, the existence of the bomber itself is threatened by the development of longer and longer range ground to ground rockets—rockets which, it is confidently predicted, will culminate in the 'intercontinental ballistic missile' within the coming decade.

These are developments in the most hideous form of warfare of all, in nuclear weapons and in the methods of their delivery upon cities as weapons of mass destruction. The question now arises inescapably whether this method of warfare has not become so overwhelming as to render all other forms of warfare relatively unimportant, at any rate in contests between great powers. Nevertheless the technical revolution proceeds in all other forms of warfare also. New applications of nuclear warfare to the operations of armies in the field follow rapidly one upon another, as 'tactical' nuclear weapons are developed. Finally the so called conventional, or non-nuclear weapons, from the fighter aircraft, through the tank and the warship, down to the rifle itself, are in constant and rapid development.

The sole tendency which can be detected as, hitherto, constant amidst this avalanche of technical change, is a tendency for the *offensive* to become more and more predominant over the *defensive*. The jet bomber of today can still conceivably be intercepted. But we are advised by the scientists and technicians that a means of either destroying or diverting the intercontinental ballistic missile of tomorrow is nowhere even in sight. This tendency for *offensive supremacy*, which appears to be irreversible as far ahead as the scientists can see, clearly raises the gravest possible issues for Defence Ministers and planners. It poses the question of whether, in the form of the intercontinental ballistic missile with hydrogen bomb warhead, 'the absolute weapon' may not be on the point of development. 'The absolute weapon' is usually defined as one which renders all other existing weapons obsolete. More broadly, the rapid contemporary development of weapons towards this point raises in the most acute form the basic question of whether 'national defence', by means of military preparations, is a policy which, however necessary it may remain in default of something better, can any longer give any nation even that measure of security which it could achieve in the past.

It is not always realised, however, that for the British defence authorities all this is only one part of the story. Not only are the technical data on which they must work in a state of 'permanent revolution', but so also are the tasks and functions of the British defence forces. The role of Britain in the world, and so the role of her forces, has changed more rapidly over the past ten years than at almost any other time in her history. From being the mistress of a world-wide dependent Empire, she is becoming one unit in an equally world-wide but voluntarily associating, Commonwealth of Nations. From being, on the whole, the leading world power, she is becoming one important but secondary member of a system of alliances.

Of these alliances, NATO is the essential, but not the only one. It is now flanked by the Baghdad and SEATO Pacts. It is the function of the other papers in this volume to discuss these arrangements. All that this paper can attempt is to point out that their existence profoundly conditions British defence policy. For the revolution in the *function* of our defence forces which these changes in the national role imply are, I think, less well realised than the aforementioned technical changes. Yet they are of at least equal importance for defence policy.

In fact, of course, the two kinds of change interlock. For example, the question of the desirability or not of the maintenance of a particular military base may be affected both by the existence of nuclear weapons and by the transformation of an Empire into a Commonwealth. In 1954 we saw this well exemplified in the case of the Suez Canal base.

In such circumstances the reader of these pages will be disappointed if he expects to find a series of suggested solutions for the defence problems with which these rapidly changing circumstances confront us. Nothing but the evolution of events will make it possible to provide such solutions. All that can be done at present is to attempt to see what are the main problems which face us, and to suggest the kind of approach which may prove fruitful. It would, after all, be a great advance if we could reach a measure of national agreement as to what are our main defence *questions*—even if no one can at this stage claim for one moment that he knows the *answers*.

The development of nuclear weapons inevitably dominates and darkens the imagination of mankind today. For the defence planners and for those on whom falls the constitutional responsibility for the defence of the British people these issues are especially acute. Is it any longer possible physically to safeguard the lives of the British people (or *mutatis mutandis* any other people) by taking military measures and making military preparations? Is this possible in anything like the same way and to anything like the same extent as could once be done by, for example, building and maintaining a dominant naval line of battle? I believe that the answer to this question, however painful it must be to face it, can only be negative. But if this is so, most important consequences for defence policy must follow. In the first place it must surely be the duty of the British Government, as of every other government, to seek for world pacification and disarmament with a quite new urgency.

Accordingly the first question that this paper must discuss is the possibility of the abolition of nuclear weapons as a part of a general disarmament convention.

It is important to realise that until recently dominant military opinion in the west was at heart hostile to any scheme for nuclear disramament, at any rate, without a corresponding degree of general disarmament, *even if genuinely effective measures of inspection and control could be secured.* (See, for example, a closely reasoned statement of this view in Marshal of the Royal Air Force Sir John Slessor's recent book *Strategy for the West.*) The reasons for this reluctance have been obvious enough. It was considered that the west had a long lead in nuclear weapons. If they were to be abolished this lead would be abolished also; worse, the equally long lead possessed by Russia in manpower would then become, it was considered, decisive. The west would have thrown away its great deterrent against the march of the Red Army. (Sir Winston Churchill in effect expressed this view by repeatedly stating that peace has been maintained by American atomic power.)

Unquestionably this contention had until recently much force. It was not possible to brush aside the considerations on which it was based, even though it involved the west in the odium of appearing to seek to preserve weapons which were by their nature more abhorrent to mankind than any other weapons which had ever been produced in human history.

The situation in which the west felt compelled to adopt this attitude has now (1956), however, changed in several important respects. First, Russia has produced effective nuclear weapons of her own, and in the case of the most deadly of these, the hydrogen bomb, appears actually to have produced a useable weapon a few months *before* America. This does not necessarily mean that the lead of the west, especially perhaps in 'tactical' nuclear weapons for use in land battles, has already disappeared. But it does indicate that that lead is, at best, a wasting asset. Moreover, it is not certain that the possession of a larger stockpile of nuclear resources, over and above some critical level (as the west, no doubt, still possesses) is a matter for much self-congratulation. Once Russia possesses sufficient hydrogen bombs to inflict unspeakably heavy damage on the west, the possession by the west not only of enough, but of twice or three times the number of bombs necessary to destroy Russia, is a rather theoretical advantage. As it has been grimly observed, in this matter of hydrogen bombs, enough may be as good as a feast. Moreover, the same sort of tendency towards an equivalence of power between Russia and the west in the means of delivering nuclear weapons is becoming apparent. On the other hand, the strength of the west in so-called 'conventional' weapons, from being pitifully small, is now becoming a little more considerable. Finally, in 1956, Russia apparently began the process of decreasing her own conventional strength.

It would, in my opinion, be premature to suggest that these develpoments would leave the balance of advantage untilted in favour of Russia if an effective arrangement for the banning of nuclear weapons, without a simultaneous reduction of 'conventional' forces, were arrived at. For the Russians still retain a very great superiority in the conventional field. The Russians are great chess players, and an elementary principle of chess is relevant to this situation. No player who is several pieces down is likely to be willing to swop queens. For his relative inferiority would be sharply increased thereby. Thus, if the nuclear weapons are the queens it cannot be denied that their exclusive elimination would still tilt the balance against the west.

This being so, it is all the more remarkable that in the early months of 1956, the western and eastern participants in the perennial disarmament discussion which goes on in the Sub-Committe of the Disarmament Commission of the United Nations largely reversed their positions. Up till then the west had proposed disarmament in the conventional field, for here Russia was the stronger; and Russia had proposed disarmament in the nuclear field, for here the west was the stronger. But now Russia abruptly accepted the western proposals for conventional disarmament, although questioning the arrangements suggested for inspection and control. The west did not respond by sticking to its proposition, subject to agreement on inspection and control. On the contrary, the western countries now took the line that nuclear disarmament—the very thing which, up till then, we had been extremely cautious over—must accompany conventional disarmament in one comprehensive convention. The Russians, it is true, did not thereupon abandon their general call for nuclear disarmament, but they now seemed to insist that conventional disarmament, the very thing which they had up till then regarded with understandable reservations, could and should precede it.

It is difficult to be greatly edified by this complicated verbal quadrille, as it is being danced at the Sub-Committee of the Disarmament Commission of the United Nations. For the successive stands taken by the west and by Russia, respectively, appear to reflect nothing so much as their respective estimates of their own and their opponent's future strengths and weaknesses in this or that sphere. Why, for example, was it necessary in 1956 for the west to deny consent to a measure of conventional disarmament (which is happening on both sides anyway) because nuclear disarmament could not be obtained simultaneously? However this present (summer 1956) phase of the disarmament negotiations will no doubt prove as transitory as have all the preceding phases; by the time these words are in their readers' hands, both the western countries and Russia may well have shifted their positions once again.

Be that as it may, it is undoubtedly true that today it would be nuclear disarmament, either complete or partial, which would really count. We must not underestimate, however, the immense difficulties to be overcome. The truth is that nuclear disarmament is something which is both supremely desirable and supremely difficult of attainment.

The main difficulty, which grows greater as time passes and stockpiles accumulate, is to secure a method of watertight and entirely reliable international inspection and control, so that no nation could retain the power individually to wage nuclear war. It is difficult to see how any convention completely abolishing nuclear weapons will be achieved unless this condition can be fulfilled. For this is a matter of life and death for each and all of the potential signatories of such a convention. No nation will enter into a disarmament convention of this sort which does not provide watertight methods for its even-handed enforcement upon all its signatories. Yet it is impossible to imagine any system of inspection and control of nuclear disarmament which would not drastically infringe the sovereignty of the nations undergoing it. To put the matter bluntly, it would involve Russians freely and continuously inspecting not only the American Strategic Air Command but also the American nuclear industry, and Americans freely and continuously inspecting the Russian Strategic Air Force and the Russain nuclear industry (and, of course, both of them doing so in the case of Britain, with Britain in turn inspecting them).

It is true that recently the American Government has offered a large measure of aerial inspection and the Russian Government has proposed inspection of another kind. And yet few people really suppose that a workable disarmament convention is about to be signed. Nevertheless the very fact that governments have begun to think in these terms at all is a sign that progress in this sphere is possible. Indeed the conclusion of some nuclear disarmament convention is in the long run so imperative if, it may well be, the human race itself is to survive, that it would be to despair to suggest that the thing is impossible. But once the realities are faced, it becomes only too clear that there is little prospect of even a measure of nuclear disarmament being easily or quickly achieved. An immense change in the whole relationship of America and Russia in particular would have to precede it, or at the very least accompany it. Nuclear disarmament could hardly be anything else but the crown and seal set upon successful efforts to achieve a general *modus vivendi* between east and west. Enthusiasts for disarmament who envisage it as a cure-all which can be applied without reference to the world situation as a whole make little useful contribution to the cause which they have at heart. For similar reasons it would be an error to despise the achievement of any step towards nuclear disarmament, however limited.

In this connection it is highly regrettable that the British Government was for some time reluctant to take the lead in attempting to negotiate a convention for the abolition, or even limitation, of further tests of nuclear weapons, and in particular nuclear fusion weapons. The weight of scientific opinion appears to be against the view that test explosions of fusion weapons at anything like the present rate (say three or four a year) are likely to have a contaminating effect upon the world's atmosphere. Nevertheless the very fact that such a possibility can be seriously discussed in scientific circles, is or ought to be, a most formidable warning to the world's statesmen that when they test the hydrogen bomb they are, in fact, testing means for the destruction of the human race and the contamination of its terrestrial home. Moreover the layman cannot fail to note that the view that test explosions are innocuous is not unanimously held by scientists, and that even the more reassuring authorities appear to agree that world contamination might well result from the number of explosions of fusion weapons which would be likely to occur in the event of an actual world war, however short in duration.

Setting aside, however, these possibilities of ultimate human catastrophe, the achievement of a convention to halt or limit further test explosions of fusion weapons would have two important advantages. First, it has the advantage of practicability. Little or no difficulty of enforcement arises. It is possible to detect immediately the detonation of a fusion weapon wherever it occurs. A convention to abolish or limit the number of such explosions would be 'self policing', in the sense that a breach of the convention would be immediately detectable to all its signatories. Therefore the nuclear powers could sign it without either, on the one hand, abrogating their sovereignty, or on the other, staking their existence on each other's good faith. Second, the achievement of even so limited and, at first sight, minor an agreement as this in the field of nuclear disarmament might well prove a turning point in world history. If even this degree of limitation could be put to the nuclear arms race, the possibility of halting the fatal progress of competitive, and therefore desperate, arming might be brought into the realm of the possible. A corner might have been turned; slow, painful and halting progress towards a lowering of the levels of armaments of the decisive kinds, instead of the present headlong race towards their apparently unlimited multiplication, might be achieved.

It is best to write frankly about the reasons which for some time prevented the British Government from taking the lead in this matter. They were, no doubt, essentially based upon the fact that Britain, unlike both America and Russia, had not yet brought her development of a fusion weapon to the point of a test detonation. Thus if further test explosions were banned she would incur an obvious relative disadvantage. There is nothing discreditable in this reasoning. It is true that if one concludes (as for reasons given below I do conclude, however reluctantly) that in default of general disarmament Britain must possess herself of fusion weapons, then clearly she must also test them.

But it is, I believe, a *non sequitur* to state that the British Government must not for these reasons attempt to secure an international convention halting or limiting further test explosions. In the first place it is only too probable that the successful negotiation of such a convention would take a long time. It might well be that this time would suffice for Britain to put herself on an equality with Russia and America in the matter. If, unexpectedly, it did not, then the British Government should have no hesitation in insisting that the coming into force of the convention should be so dated that an opportunity for Britain to conduct the necessary minimum tests would be afforded. Nor should the British Government feel any difficulty in stating frankly the reasons why this was necessary to her.

It is therefore, satisfactory that, in the first half of 1956, Her Majesty's Government joined with the French Government in proposing that a convention limiting or abolishing further test explosions of fusion weapons should be negotiated—and, significantly, in the same period, announced that a British fusion weapon would be tested in the first half of 1957. What is not so satisfactory is that the British Government has so far failed to make the conclusion of such a convention a major object of British policy—to insist upon it in season and out of season, to give world opinion a true lead in this matter. For once the realities are honestly faced there is nothing in the least contradictory in insisting on making one's own tests, and yet, at the same time, proposing that, since the other two nuclear powers have already made theirs, the making of all further rests should be limited or prohibited. For so long as the indispensable condition that Britain is not put in a position of permanent inferiority to those nations which have already made their tests is satisfied, it would be enormously to the interest of Britain to secure even this limitation to the nuclear arms race. It is true that America, Russia and Britain would still be able to increase indefinitely their respective stockpiles of fusion weapons. But, for the reasons given above, once each was possessed of a stockpile of a certain rather limited size, there would be little incentive to do so. For at that stage each would know that she could both completely destroy and be destroyed by, the others with the existing stock. It is probable, indeed, that such a convention as this would in the end either develop into a much more effective form of disarmament or break down. But that is true of almost all possible methods of halting this present competitive race towards the point of no return for our species.

It follows, however, from these reflections upon the difficulty of taking even the above modest first step that it is quite impossible to plan British defence policy upon the assumption of an early achievement of general nuclear disarmament. What future British governments could do—and that would be much —would be to make this achievement the supreme long term goal for which they worked unremittingly; what future British governments could do is to abandon the reservations which their predecessors, like other western governments, have made even to the initial steps towards such an achievement. But even with the best will in the world on both sides, nuclear, as a part of general, disarmament will remain a supremely difficult thing to achieve in practice. It must be the goal towards which we work. But it would be folly to suppose that we had already reached that goal.

Hitherto successive British governments have considered that, in default of their abolition as a part of general disarmament, Britain must possess fission and fusion nuclear weapons and the means of delivering them.

In default of nuclear disarmament the decision reached by the Labour government to develop, and by the Conservative government to persevere with, nuclear weapons can only be challenged, it seems, upon two assumptions. It can be, and of course is, challenged on absolute pacifist assumptions; but that assumption also challenges all other defence policies and cannot, therefore be discussed within the framework of a paper devoted to the question of what should be the character of British defence policy. The decision of successive British governments to equip Britain with nuclear weapons can also be challenged, however, on the assumption that these 'super-weapons' are both unnecessary and repugnant for the purposes of British defence. It can be argued that, even though it is necessary for Britain to maintain adequate ground, sea and air forces, yet it is wrong for a power of medium size such as Britain to provide itself with the 'super-weapons'. It is suggested that the type of defence forces needed by Britain are infantry for such operations as those in Korea and Malaya, the smaller naval craft for anti-submarine purposes, defensive fighter aircraft and defensive ground to air guided missiles. The large sums now being devoted to nuclear weapons and strategic bombers could, it is suggested, be saved.

This must be a most attractive policy for any British Chancellor of the Exchequer. But it is important to envisage clearly the role to which its adoption would assign Britain. The role of a Britain equipped with such defence forces could hardly be (as appears to be sometimes envisaged) that of a detached spectator of the major world tensions. The fact is that, in order to play any such role as that (if it ever becomes a practical possibility) a greater rather than a lesser degree of British power would surely be needed. The more independence of policy is aimed at, the less, not the more, possible it would be for a British government to reduce Britain to the relative impotence to which the unilateral abolition of nuclear weapons must inevitably condemn a nation today. For no scientific or military authority has ever been able to promise us even the possibility of watertight—or rather 'atom-tight'—defence. Therefore capacity to hold one's own in the contemporary world must largely depend upon *the capacity to deter a potential assailant*. And if that is a highly desirable requirement even for a member of an alliance such as NATO, it would be an essential requirement for a completely independent nation. Yet such capacity to deter can alone be provided by the possession of nuclear weapons and the capacity to deliver them. To sum up the point: whether or not the world situation may some day evolve in such a way that this country would become more detached from the major power-groups than it is today is a highly debatable question. But if such an evolution does take place, the need for the possession of nuclear weapons by Britain will almost certainly be felt more, rather than less, strongly than it is today.

The only national role for which the abandonment of nuclear weapons by Britain would be appropriate would be, on the contrary, a role of one of the subsidiary allies of the United States— an ally, moreover, whose weakness would give her little or no influence. If Britain should ever become content with a position in which she would not seriously attempt either to be an independent factor in the balance of world forces, or even to influence her major ally, and so the course of world events, the savings to be derived from the scrapping of our nuclear weapons and strategic bombers could be realised. But the fact should be faced that in that event, far from having contracted out of the main power tensions, we should have become wholly dependent upon American nuclear weapons. To put the point in the most concrete form possible, by avoiding the existence of British nuclear bombs and bombers on our airfields, we should inevitably perpetuate the presence there of American nuclear bombs and bombers. It is doubtful whether all of the advocates of the abandonment of nuclear weapons by Britain have thought this issue through.

Again, simplicity and frankness are indispensable as to the real motives which prompt us to support (always in default of the achievement of nuclear disarmament) the development of British nuclear weapons and the means of delivering them. These motives are broadly that without these weapons Britain, this highly vulnerable island, would be unable to exercise independent influence upon the course of world events. She would always, in the last resort, have to defer to her enemies, or to her allies. For those who do not believe that Britain has now any particular role to play in the world that may be a tolerable prospect. But for those of us who have a profound faith in Britain and in the value of British stability, sanity and experience, the eclipse of the capacity of Britain to pursue, if necessary, an independent policy at critical junctures would be a betrayal of some of the highest hopes of humanity. No doubt such independence of policy is a relative thing. It is hard to imagine a situation in which Britain could pursue a policy without allies and associates. But there is nothing new in that situation. Britain has been a member of alliances, and has been in that sense dependent upon allies, for much the longer part of her history. But there is all the difference in the world between working with allies while we possess the ultimate capacity, if no longer to defend ourselves effectively (it is doubtful if any nation any longer possesses that), yet to deter attack upon us; there is all the difference in the world between membership of such self-respecting alliances, and subsiding into the position of a helpless satellite. These are the reasons which compel the conclusion that, in default of measures of general nuclear disarmament, it is impossible to advocate the reversal of existing British defence policy in the all important respect of the development of nuclear weapons.

We may now examine the opposite question. If in default of general disarmament, we have got to have nuclear weapons, can we not at least dispense with some or all of our existing 'conventional' weapons? If nuclear weapons are now of so decisive a character that we dare not be without them, until and unless we can secure an international agreement for their abolition, what, it may be asked, is the use of spending hundreds of millions of pounds on the older type of armaments?

Unfortunately for future Chancellors of the Exchequer, this argument overlooks some of the most important functions for which British defence forces are required. If we had only to consider the problem of how to deter a potential aggressor from a third world war, then the above argument would have some force (although even then it would be an over-simplification). But in fact, of course, British armed forces have at least two other roles to fulfil in addition to acting as a deterrent. They are used as the Commonwealth police force. And they are also used in the 'small wars', such as Korea, which, so far, have punctuated the post-1945 period.

The extent to which we should continue to use them in these roles will be discussed below. But until and unless we can curtail our present commitments in these respects, we must provide defence forces of an adequate type and size for the tasks which we give them. And it so happens that nuclear weapons are unsuited to either of these two functions.

In the case of 'Korea type' wars, the use of nuclear weapons is no doubt possible; but in the almost unanimous opinion of responsible statesmen and their military advisers (some United States Air and Sea general officers dissenting), it would be highly undesirable. To use even tactical nuclear weapons for such a purpose (unless they are used against us) approaches the doctrine of 'massive mobile retaliation'. And it is now widely recognised that this doctrine would be likely to lead, in practice, straight towards turning any future small war into a third world war. It is now generally agreed that, if the world is to escape destruction, the west must be in a position to assert a *local and limited* degree of armed power at particular points where it may be needed. For this purpose 'conventional' land, sea and air forces are necessary. Unless we want to risk turning every Korea into a world war, or alternatively to have no means of preventing local aggression, we have still got to have the older types of arms.

It is true that a new doctrine has recently (1955) been propounded in this connection, notably and earnestly by Admiral Sir Anthony Buzzard, sometime Director of Naval Intelligence. This is the doctrine of 'graduated deterrence' by which it is suggested that a sort of scale of retaliation shall be 'established' by the west, and by which in particular the west should 'establish' the right to use tactical atomic weapons in 'Korea type' wars without incurring reprisal from the Communist bloc in the form of hydrogen bomb attacks on ourselves. No doubt it would be highly desirable for the west to 'establish' such a principle. But for that very reason it is difficult to name any reason which would make it probable that the Communist powers would concur in it. Nevertheless the underlying *conception* that the west should apply the minimum amount of force, and no more, that any particular situation demands is undoubtedly correct and highly important. Any other principle, such as the original conception of massive mobile retaliation—i.e. the threat to use the hydrogen bomb to counter every local encroachment or aggression—is far too dangerous to be practicable. But the determination to resist local and limited aggression by local and limited applications of force entails the maintenance of forces which are capable of such local and limited use. This is the first reason why the maintenance of conventional forces is still, unfortunately, indispensable.

For the purpose of the 'Commonwealth police' function, conventional armaments are still more necessary. It is true that it is highly desirable progressively to divest ourselves of the burden of this function, by completing the transformation of the former British Empire into a voluntarily associating Commonwealth, the members of which will provide for their own internal security. Fortunately this process is going on very fast. By far the greater part of what was the colonial empire in 1945 has already become self-governing and self-policing. Nevertheless it would be unrealistic to suggest that we can quickly complete the process in the case of all the remaining non-self-governing colonies, amongst which are, naturally, some of the less developed areas. Therefore unless we are willing to allow a few thousand well-organised Communists to take over the government of Malaya, for example, (which I have always thought they have no more right to rule than we have), instead of developing genuine democratic self-government there, as we are doing, we must have the services of our patient, long suffering, British infantry battalions. For nuclear weapons are simply irrelevant to such a requirement. In a word, unless we are willing to be at the mercy of any well-led and ruthless group which aspires to usurp the government of any paritcular part of the still non-self-governing Commonwealth, we have an undeniable continuing requirement, above all for well disciplined infantry.

The above conclusions, if they are valid, are in themselves sufficiently grave. If it cannot be denied that Britain's present role in the world requires of her an adequate provision of both nuclear and conventional weapons, the prospect before the Treasury (in default of an acceptable international agreement on disarmament) is a bleak one. Unfortunately, however, this is not all. Over and above the requirements of the armed forces there looms the question of Civil Defence.

The basic decisions which future British governments will have to take upon the question of civil defence are, I believe, among the most perplexing in the whole defence field. It is to make no party point to say that no one can be satisfied with the present position. In 1954, for example, we proposed to spend some £40 million on civil defence, and actually spent about £29 million. This is quite a large sum to devote to one particular item in the general defence budget. On the other hand, nothing could be clearer than that it is not providing us with anything which could even remotely be called protection against nuclear attack.

Anyone who has any familiarity with the realities of nuclear attack by fusion weapons is tempted to suggest that the whole civil defence effort should be abandoned as having become hopeless. It is an undeniable fact which had better be faced that, if a nuclear war on a world scale in which Britain was a belligerent actually broke out, our country would almost certainly receive damage such as we have never even contemplated before in our history, whatever course of action we take now. Nevertheless we argued above that in default of an effective general disarmament agreement, the case for the retention by us of nuclear weapons was conclusive, not because we could necessarily save ourselves by their use if once war broke out, but because their possession constituted the one effective *deterrent* to an attack upon these islands with which we could provide ourselves.

A similar argument can be used in the case of civil defence. If it is true that a potential assailant of this island will be deterred by the knowledge that we possess nuclear weapons with which we could and should inflict perhaps mortal retaliatory damage upon him, is it not also true that his temptation to attack us will be *pro tanto* diminished if we have provided ourselves with civil defences which can offer a prospect at least of preserving the lives of some of the citizens of our great cities in the event of nuclear attack? In a word, if strength in the nuclear field is indispensable to us in order to avoid attack, is it not also at least useful to possess some defensive as well as offensive strength? Surely we must conclude that it is.

The only question is, however, as to whether any measures of large scale civil defence would, in fact, appreciably increase our defensive strength against hydrogen bomb attack. At one time I was inclined to consider that they might, and that it might consequently be our national duty to face the truly gigantic task of attempting to provide real civil defences, including deep shelters for the tens of millions of people who inhabit our great cities. After studying the problem to the best of my ability, and having visited and inspected the Swedish civil defence installations (which are much the most extensive and advanced in the world), I have come to the view that it is technically impossible to provide an appreciable degree of shelter against hydrogen bomb attack for the population of our great cities. The insuperable problem is that of the lack of warning time. In these circumstances, the many hundreds of millions of pounds which our attempt to construct deep shelters would have cost may not after all fall upon our defence budget. But this is not to say that we can possibly leave civil defence in its present condition. No government which takes its defence programme seriously can avoid incurring appreciable annual expenditure on civil defence, if only on the provision of mobile columns and rescue work of various kinds. Again, essential military and civil installations may well have to be provided with deep shelters and even this would be an exceedingly costly business. Therefore, we must face the fact that our defence budget will have to carry appreciable civil defence expenditures.

We are immediately faced with the other side of the defence question. If we are forced to the conclusion that we need each of the above types of defence, namely nuclear weapons, conventional arms, and civil defence, we must at once ask whether we can possibly afford them. We must consider the question of cost.

People often tend to fly from one extreme to the other on this question of defence costs. Those who are temperamentally opposed to defence spending often describe our present defence spending (some £1,500 million a year) as 'ruinous', 'crushing', and 'certain to lead us to national bankruptcy'. Those who feel acutely the need of adequate defence are, on the other hand, apt to brush aside all questions of cost. They feel that the country 'must have' completely adequate defences at all points, and tend to neglect the fact that it is not much use to defend a country which cannot pay its way.

The only way to introduce a sense of proportion into this controversy, which is too often conducted on a highly emotional level, is to cite the basic figures involved. Fortunately they are few and simple. The first thing to keep in mind is that what matters is not so much the absolute amount of our defence expenditure, or even its size compared with the rest of the Government's expenditure (the total budget), as the *proportion* which our defence spending bears to our total national income. What matters is how much of all the wealth produced each year for all purposes we have to devote to defence. What matters, to put it personally, is how many shillings in the pound each one of us has, on the average, to devote to defence instead of to all our other purposes, both private and public. This way of looking at the matter will immediately enable us to get our present level of defence spending of some £1,500 million a year into perspective. Our national income for all purposes in 1955 was £16,634 million and our defence expenditure £1,505 million. Thus we see that we were devoting about 9 per cent of all our resources to defence.

When people who have not hitherto studied this problem first realise these facts they are apt to jump to the conclusion that a defence budget of some £1,500 million is not such a very heavy burden after all. And it is true that our nation is not going to be 'ruined', 'crushed', or 'driven into national bankruptcy' by devoting some 10 per cent of its resources (2s. in the pound) to defence. If we continue to have to do so, all that will happen is that, other things being equal, we shall all be 10 per cent poorer than we otherwise might have been.

On the other hand, a 10 per cent defence expenditure is a good deal more serious a matter from an economic standpoint than it might appear to be. It is certainly not something to be tolerated except as a matter of absolute necessity. Ten per cent of the total national income is a much heavier burden than it may sound, because so high a proportion of our productive resources *must* be used for two or three other indispensable purposes. For instance, in order to sustain a tolerable standard of life we must consume the biggest part of all that we produce. Second, a substantial part must be exported in order to pay for our food and raw materials. Third, we ought, on pain of falling behind our competitors, to use something like a fifth of all we produce for new capital development and the maintenance of our existing productive equipment. Finally, there are our 'social' expenditures—education, the social services—which it is also not only highly desirable, but in the modern world an actual necessity, to undertake. Therefore to devote even 10 per cent of our total productive resources to defence is, after all, a very serious matter. For it represents far more than a tithe of that *margin* of our resources which is available after we have satisfied claims on them which cannot be gainsaid.

The truth is, then, that, while it is wrong to say that we *cannot* stand some £1,500 million a year of defence expenditure, yet the burden of it is very heavy since it seriously curtails our ability to do other highly desirable things, such as rapid capital and social development. Our verdict must surely be that our present level of defence spending is very high and that it is urgently desirable, to put the matter no more strongly, to reduce it to substantially below 10 per cent of the national income.

We have reviewed above, however, our two main categories of defence expenditure—conventional and nuclear weapons— and we have been driven to the conclusion that, in default of an effective international agreement on the limitation of armaments, we cannot dispense with either of them. The question is how can we possibly do all this and at the same time get the total bill substantially below 10 per cent of the national income? Never has the task of balancing requirements and resources in the defence field been more difficult.

Future Chancellors of the Exchequer, Ministers of the defence departments, and defence planners must surely seek for the solution in one of two fields. Either they must succeed in the extremely difficult task of achieving a general disarmament convention, which will abolish nuclear weapons and limit other forms of armament also, or in default of that they must look for economies in the field of conventional armaments. We have seen that we cannot possibly do without conventional armaments, however much of our resources we are forced to devote to nuclear warfare. But that is not to say that we cannot substantially curtail our expenditure upon, in particular, the Army and the Royal Navy. Air Force expenditure is, of course, itself bound up with nuclear warfare, though here also the trend of technical development may afford us the opportunity of considerable economies. We may conclude this paper by looking very briefly at the three Services in turn.

The Army

The British Army today has two main functions. First, it has to provide a contingent in the NATO forces in Europe. The present Conservative Government (1956) has perpetuated, although not, it is fair to say, increased, this commitment, which amounts to four divisions. There is no doubt that this commitment is still necessary. But it is necessary for rather different reasons from those for which it was at first undertaken. It would be unrealistic to think that the NATO land and air forces deployed in Europe are today the decisive factor in deterring a Russian invasion of the west. That decisive factor is provided by the ability of the west to deliver hydrogen bombs upon Russian targets. It is not offset by the Russian ability to do likewise. It would be truer to say that there now exists a mutual deterrent of the most formidable kind.

The role of the NATO ground and air forces has become the more modest one of providing a screen, or as Sir John Slessor has expressed it 'a trip wire',* which prevents the over-running or, more realistically perhaps, the overawing of western Europe without world war. For the present at least they are indispensable for that function. But their constitution, armaments and organisation might be reconsidered in the light of a realisation that this is their function. For example, is it any longer realistic to think in terms of a long ground war, lasting over years, fought, no doubt, with tactical nuclear weapons but on a modernised version of 1945 methods? Is it not more realistic to envisage that any future world war would be decided (and decided by mutual destruction) far above the heads of the armies, and decided in hours, days, weeks or at most months rather than years?

Second, the British Army must provide ground forces both to be available against the contingency of limited wars of the Korean type, in order to stop aggression on the spot, and for police type operations in the still dependent parts of the Commonwealth such as Malaya. For these purposes we entered in the immediate post-war years into widespread and substantial overseas commitments—nearly a division in Korea, a division in Hong Kong, some twenty battalions in Malaya, a brigade in Kenya, a brigade in Trieste, and no less than three divisions in Egypt.

Fortunately these appallingly onerous, widespread, and, above all, distant commitments are now (1956) at last being reduced. Korea has been reduced to one battalion, and so has Kenya; the Malayan commitment is at last easing, our forces in Trieste have

*In a lecture entitled *Germany and the Defence of the West*, delivered in Berlin, January 1956.

been withdrawn, and finally all three divisions have been withdrawn from Egypt (although approximately one will be retained in the Middle East). This is a veritable revolution in the distant overseas commitments of the British Army.

It was in 1950 that the period of national service was put up to its present (1956) extremely high level of two years. It is important to realise that this was done because such an extension of the period of national service was the sole possible way of providing men for our *distant* overseas commitments, which had been suddenly increased by the need to keep a substantial number of men, and to keep them fighting, at the other end of the world in Korea. It was this Korean commitment, coming on the top of all our distant commitments, which made the two year period inevitable. For it would have been impossibly wasteful to have used units containing a high proportion of national service men at the other side of the world, if these men had served for only one year or even for eighteen months; an impossibly high proportion of their time would have been spent in transit.

Therefore the key to a reduction in the period of national service lies in the reduction of those distant commitments, and fortunately it is just these that are now being reduced. The 1954 commitment to Germany, whether or not we think it justified on other grounds, does not in itself present us with an insurmountable obstacle to a reduction in the period of service. For the transit time of moving a man to north-west Germany is relatively negligible.

A reduction in the period of national service from two years to eighteen months would reduce the size of the Army (other things being equal) by some 50,000 men and the total size of the armed forces by some 80,000 men. Some such reduction as this in the total manpower which we devote to our 'conventional' forces is the very least that we can do if we are to be able to afford the other types of defence effort which, as we have seen, are so necessary to us.

This is not to say that a reduction in the period of national service to, say, eighteen months would be an easy matter for the Army to contemplate. Even with the partial liquidation of its distant overseas commitments which is now taking place, a re-

duction of six months in the period served by a national service
man, with its loss of 50,000 men with the colours, would set the
Army some extremely difficult problems. In particular it would
make more difficult the achievement of an important aim which
successive chiefs of the Imperial General Staff have cherished
ever since 1945, namely the establishment of an effective strategic reserve in the United Kingdom. On the other hand, it
would be too much to say that it would make the establishment
of such an effective strategic reserve impossible. Much would
depend upon the rate of recruiting to and of extension and re-
engagement in, the regular Army—as well as on the course of
events in our remaining overseas commitments.

There is little doubt that by far the most economical arrangement would be for our remaining *distant* commitments to be
undertaken by units wholly or largely composed of relatively
long service regulars, while national service men were used in
north-west Germany and to form the bulk of the strategic reserve at home. But any such arrangement as this in turn raises
most difficult problems, such as those of varying the national
service content of different units and of the provision of senior
NCO's and warrant officers in sufficient numbers

Nevertheless the need to reduce the period of national service
from the present level of two years will become more and more
pressing. A two year period was never contemplated as a permanent feature of our national life when it was introduced in
1950. On the contrary, the Ministers for the defence departments in the Labour Government then in office (of which I was
one) gave binding assurance to the House that this would be
only a temporary and emergency measure. After the conclusion
of the Korean war, and also after the commitment to keep
troops in Korea has been reduced to very small proportions, it
is increasingly difficult to justify perpetuating the infliction of
this very heavy burden upon the youth of the nation.

The truth is that the whole question of the reduction of the
period of national service has now become a secondary one. The
scheme adopted by the Government in 1955 for the postpone-
ment of the timing of the call up by stages from 18 to 19 years,
and the cessation of the call up of Grade III men, will actually
decrease the number of national service men available to the

forces by more than a reduction of the period of service by six months would do. In other words it would be perfectly possible, by cancelling the present Government scheme, and reverting to the age of 18 for the call up, to obtain more men, not less, and yet to reduce the period of service to eighteen months. Undoubtedly there are military disadvantages in the shorter period. But, after all, eighteen months was the period of service up till 1950. It is hardly possible to claim, therefore, that it is unworkable.

The question of the future of national service is a perplexing one. The truth is that a *short* period of national service, on a permanent basis, is a most unattractive proposition from a strictly defence standpoint. No worse system could be imagined for forces faced with our two main requirements of a nuclear deterrent and limited conventional forces. Clearly what is needed for both those functions are relatively small, highly trained and equipped, and, above all, long service *professional* forces. These obvious considerations have made some professional service opinion consider carefully whether the outright abolition of national service and the substitution for it of far more attractive pay and conditions for our regular, long service, professional forces is not, on strictly defence grounds, the only final solution to our problem. I do not myself doubt that this is so. On the other hand, the difficulties of any immediate abandonment of national service cannot be ignored. There is the whole question of providing sufficiently attractive pay and conditions of service to *ensure* that the present profoundly unsatisfactory rate of regular recruiting is raised to one which will provide (and provide in terms of 'man-years' of service—the length of engagement and re-engagement is just as important a question as that of recruitment) professional forces of, say, at least the same order of magnitude as we used to possess before the Second World War. (The 1955–6 increase in pay may have dealt with one side of the problem. But it has not touched equally important factors such as accommodation.)

There is, also, the whole question of the psychological effect of opinion, both at home and abroad, of a British decision to abolish national service. Public opinion has, as yet, so little realised the true characteristics and requirements of nuclear warfare, and the true role of British forces in the world of today, that a decision which would in fact have the effect of greatly strengthening British power, by concentrating our effort at the decisive point, might well be regarded as a grave weakening of that power. Nor can such psychological factors, irritating and frustrating as they are, be brushed aside. It may be as important to be thought strong as to be strong. Nevertheless, in the long run, there is no substitute for the *fact* of strength. The amount of the national effort available for defence purposes must, I repeat, be got down to well below 10 per cent of the national income, because of the considerations discussed above. For these reasons I have become convinced that precisely in order to assure an essential degree of strength in the two decisive spheres (i.e. nuclear deterrence and 'fire brigade' conventional forces), we must stop the dispersion of our effort involved in maintaining such institutions as national service, which provide a type of force which is no longer appropriate to our needs.

In my opinion it will be necessary to work out a scheme for the abolition of national service at a given date. In 1956, for example, we should plan to have the last call up in, say, 1958. This would mean that the last national service men would leave the Colours in 1959 (if the period of service was eighteen months). The period during which national service was being run down would give time for an increased flow of regular recruiting to have its effect. Moreover if any given level of pay and conditions were evidently proving inadequate to provide the necessary flow of recruits, there would be time to improve them to whatever extent became necessary to attract and hold the indispensable number of men. Nevertheless, it may well prove impossible to recruit on regular engagement more than enough men to maintain an army of the same approximate size as existed before national service, say 180,000–200,000 men. With this sized regular force on the ground we must be content, and must not undertake more commitments than can be met by it.

The Royal Navy

Decisions of a far-reaching character must sooner or later be faced in regard to the Royal Navy. But here again this paper can do no more than list the chief issues which appear to confront us. Is the Navy's continued reliance on the big ship—with all that it implies by way of 'overheads' in shore facilities—even if the big ship now takes the form of the carrier instead of the battleship—still justified in the nuclear age? And linked with that issue, what is the proper form for the control and command of the sea?

This latter question raises the whole issue of the relationship between the Royal Navy and the Royal Air Force. Mr. James Callaghan, in the debate on the 1954 Naval Estimates, suggested (with support from both sides of the House) that the only final solution might ultimately be found to lie in the actual amalgamation of the two Services. A more immediate proposal might be that the Fleet Air Arm and Coastal Command of the R.A.F. should be amalgamated under some form of joint control. No doubt such a proposal might have to carry with it something in the nature of 'interlocking directorates' between the Air Council and the Board of Admiralty. But such integration at the top might not face the same degree of human resistance as would full amalgamation.

The Royal Air Force

The Royal Air Force is, for the time being at least, the chief vehicle for the delivery of nuclear weapons. As such it seems inevitable that our defence effort will have to concentrate more and more upon it. It would, however, be a mistake to suppose that the technical revolution necessarily indicates that *all* parts of the Royal Air Force should be equally emphasised. That, at any rate, is not the opinion of some of our leading authorities on air warfare. For example, Air Chief Marshal Sir Hugh Pughe Lloyd, writing in the Aviation Supplement of *The Times* for September 18th, 1955, makes a case—which it is difficult to refute—for a high degree of concentration of effort upon the bomber element within the R.A.F. itself. He writes:

In this age of the bomber and thermo-nuclear weapons the extreme vulnerability of this island of ours is an appalling thought. It is highly populated and some areas have particularly high densities of population. Twenty hydrogen bombs or a few more, or even considerably less, and that would be the end of us. Of course, our defences would exact a heavy toll, but it would make no appreciable difference to the result; that is, the desired number of the right types of bombs would be delivered on the targets as planned, to achieve the desired and mortal effect. The only defence against a bomber is another bomber. Our only defence is to have in our hands so terrifying and devastating a bomber force to strike an instant and mortal blow that it will deter the enemy and force him to hold back.

Unless and until the Air Chief Marshal's argument can be effectively refuted, it is difficult to avoid drawing some extremely drastic conclusions from it. We are expending an enormous effort, in terms not only of money and of men, but also in terms of desperately scarce scientific skill and of highly skilled labour, not only upon naval and military weapons designed for the old type of 'hot war' between great powers, but also upon fighter aircraft, both in their tactical role with the Army and in their role of the air defence of Great Britain, and also on the aircraft of Coastal Command and of the Fleet Air Arm. At the same time we are making desperately slow progress with the development of our strategical force of V bombers. For they have to compete with all the other arms for money, men, scientific skill and skilled labour.

Yet if Air Chief Marshal Sir Hugh Pughe Lloyd's view is correct, the diversion of some at least of these scarce resources to the development of our V bomber fleet would give us far greater security, in the only way that security can now be provided, namely by way of the creation of a really effective deterrent. In fact, the strictly logical conclusion which might be drawn from Sir Hugh Pughe Lloyd's thesis, taken literally, would be that we ought to concentrate wholly upon our deterrent bomber fleet as a security against the outbreak of hot war, and in addition to provide ourselves merely with the 'conventional' land, sea and air forces suitable for cold war purposes as defined above!

No doubt no one could in practice drive the logic of the situation quite so far as that. For example, it is clearly imperative to look ahead to the time when the day of the bomber also will have passed, and therefore to provide ample resources for the development of guided missiles of all sorts, including the longest range rockets. Nevertheless the most searching reconsideration of our whole defence programme is surely overdue. Nor must we flinch, at this extraordinary moment, from conclusions which would have seemed fantastic even a few years ago.

Summary and Conclusions

In such a situation no more than general and in many respects tentative conclusions can be drawn. Nevertheless, certain facts seem to stand out starkly. We shall surely ignore them at our peril.

First. The technical revolution in warfare has now reached a point at which no effective defence against nuclear attack is possible.

Second. At this point warfare changes its character and the only long term hope for the continuance of organised human life on the planet becomes some method of abolishing large scale war employing nuclear weapons. Advance towards this goal becomes the only British defence policy which can bring real security to the British people.

Third. The difficulties in the way of effective advance along these lines must not, however, be underestimated. An interim defence policy for Britain, during the period before nuclear weapons have been effectively abolished, is indispensable.

Fourth. During this period Britain must possess nuclear weapons and the means of delivering them.

Fifth. This raises the most acute problems as to the proper division of the limited defence effort available.

Sixth. It is necessary to maintain 'conventional' weapons for local wars, and Commonwealth police purposes.

Seventh. Examination of our present defence effort shows, however, that we are devoting very large resources to providing conventional weapons apparently designed for the extremely unlikely event of a global war between great powers in which nuclear weapons were not used, or were used only in a tactical role, while relatively starving our nuclear deterrent.

Eighth. Expert evidence upon the impossibility of defence

against nuclear attack points towards the conclusion that our defence effort ought to be increasingly devoted to

    (a) the creation of a really effective nuclear deterrent, and

    (b) the maintenance of conventional forces for local war and Commonwealth police purposes only.

IV

THE MIDDLE EAST

T. E. M. McKITTERICK

THE Middle East is a perfect case-study in the application—or misapplication—of most of the main principles in international politics as they are practised today. It is an area where the west has obvious strategic and economic interests. Power politics, played by outside countries over the corpse of the Ottoman Empire, have done much to determine the course of its history. Present troubles are due in large measure to the response of non-European peoples to European intrusion. The case of Israel shows up the limitations of collective security when it is invoked to authorise a change rather than to protect the *status quo*. And finally, the whole course of western relations with the Middle East in the last half century at least shows how very wrong the Foreign Offices of the western countries can sometimes be.

It is of the essence of tragedy that the *peripeteia*, the fall that comes after pride, should be brought about partly by the fault of the central figure. In the period between the wars, France and Britain held the stage of Middle Eastern politics. The second World War saw the ultimate catastrophe of French policy, culminating in the half-ludicrous, half-tragic moment in May 1945 when British troops were used to restrain the French from bombarding the centre of Damascus; the train of events that led to that episode can be followed along its consistent course from the Versailles Conference onwards, so that in retrospect it is perfectly obvious why it happened. But if 1945 was the end of a French policy, what is one to say about Britain's position in the ten years following? The rejection by Iraq of the Treaty of Portsmouth in 1948, the Palestine war, Abadan, Suez, Cyprus— all these are no less milestones on a downward path, and the *denouement* of 1955 when Egypt accepted arms from a Communist supplier and began to organise an anti-western military grouping under Soviet auspices, was none the less tragic; for this revival of the Eastern Question was the end of a British policy over a century old, and forced the Government (and the American Administration) into an 'agonising reappraisal' which ought to have have been made several years earlier. The difference between the French and British tragedies is that, while France can be condemned in retrospect for things that were done in the unenlightened days before 1939, Britain suffered from no lack of well informed and well disposed critics of her policy after 1945. If in the end that policy faces disaster, it is at least partly because the critics were not heeded.*

There is nothing surprising in the current revival of Soviet interest in the Middle East—except that it did not take place much earlier. What was done in 1955 was in accord with all the best principles of power politics, and since Britain and France before the second World War, and Britain and America after it, had been playing a very similar sort of power politics their indignation at the appearance of a new competitor could be expected to raise no general international sympathy. The west had lived for too long under the comfortable illusion that the Eastern Question had been settled once for all in 1918 with the final collapse of the Ottoman Empire and the forced withdrawal from the scene of a revolutionary Russia and a defeated Germany. When it arose in its new form (not without warning, since the episodes of Azerbaijan in 1946 and the Straits in 1947 were fully in line with Russia's secular policy) it was all the more serious because the Middle East was no longer merely a line of communication and a strategic jumping-off point, but an area of the greatest economic importance.

Both strategic necessities and the presence of oil in large quantities are commonly adduced as arguments for preserving as much as possible of the western 'position' in the Middle East. These are the great 'interests' to which, in the conventional approach, practically all else must be subordinated. Before trying to pass judgment on them, or on the policies that flow from them, both arguments call for close examination.

First, the strategic argument. Western concern with the narrow strip of land separating the Mediterranean from the Red

*This chapter was already in print when President Nasser's nationalisation of the Suez Canal was announced.

Sea and the Indian Ocean is as old as trade with the Spice Islands, was intensified in the eighteenth century when India came under French and British control, and was elevated into a cardinal principle of policy when the Suez Canal was opened. There were traditionally two main routes, the one following the line where the Canal now is, the other through Turkey, Aleppo and the Euphrates valley to the ports of the Persian Gulf; the first came virtually under British protection after the Battle of the Nile, the second was the one that interested Germany most, at the time of the Baghdad Railway project. A large part of the old Eastern Question concerned the trade routes; what was to happen to them when the Ottoman Empire collapsed? After fighting one war and threatening another in order to exclude Russia from the approaches to the Indian Ocean and the eastern Mediterranean, Britain suddenly reversed her policy in 1907 when, as the price for an alliance against Germany, she agreed to a Russian sphere of influence in Persia. In 1915, in order to keep the alliance warm, Constantinople was allocated to Russia as part of the spoils of victory, and in 1916 the Sykes-Picot agreement partitioned the eastern Ottoman lands between Britain, Russia and France. Only the Russian revolution saved the other two allies from having to redeem promises which, if intended to be redeemed, made nonsense of fifty years of strategic argument, and if not, were an egregious piece of duplicity.

The strategic argument in its modern form does not rest so much on the importance of the Middle East as a line of communication. In the late war, a successful (though extremely costly) campaign was conducted in the area even though control of the central Mediterranean had been lost, and the Far Eastern theatre was also kept supplied round the Cape. One presumes, also, that in a future war air transport will be used a great deal more than in the last one, and it is easier to find suitable sites for airfields than for ports. In any case, in a full-scale war in which atomic and thermo-nuclear weapons were being used, the Suez Canal could be put out of action by a single bomb and the port of Basra by another.

The case for continued strategic interest rests rather on the principle that access to the Red Sea and the Persian Gulf should be denied to a possible enemy. That was one of the objects of the

Crimean War and of the constant efforts made by Britain in the late nineteenth century to exclude Russia from Persia and Mesopotamia; it was also one of the reasons why, in 1946, Britain and America insisted on the withdrawal of Soviet troops from Persian Azerbaijan. There is absolutely no doubt that direct Russian access to ports anywhere in southern Asia would transform the character of war at sea, and would place the western powers at a considerable disadvantage in supplying any theatre of war fronting on the Indian Ocean. Thus, so long as we are thinking in terms of possible major wars against Russia, there appears at first sight to be a sound strategic argument for wanting to keep the Middle East at least neutral and to give it some hope that its neutrality will be respected.

In terms of major wars, there seems to be a stronger case still for seeking to retain western influence in at least a few key areas between the Mediterranean and India, since the whole region is within comparatively easy bombing range (or guided missile range) of some of the most important industrial areas of the Soviet Union. If the Middle East is to be used as a jumping-off ground in this way, neutrality is not enough; some at least of the states must be actually allied to the western powers, and must be prepared to permit the western powers to build and maintain bases on their territory in peacetime. The Suez Canal zone was such a base, Cyprus is one now, and so is the American base at Dhahran which is held on a short-term lease from the Saudi Arabian government. The strategic objection to them is, of course, that each of them could be put out of action as easily as the Suez Canal or Basra. Effective missile-launching sites would have to be secret, and would lose their value once they were discovered.

There is a fourth approach to the strategic argument, which does not think in terms of major wars at all. The Middle East is one of the areas which might at some stage become the scene of the sort of local disturbance that current military thinking believes to be possible without involving full-scale action by the great powers. In such a case it would be most important for the west to see that the supply of oil was not affected; indeed, almost any type of disturbance in or near the oil countries could be regarded as a threat to western interests. It could also conceivably happen that the west might wish to intervene in one of the Middle Eastern countries to prevent the setting up of a government which would take the country into the other camp; British troops were actually used in this way several times between the wars, and on at least three important occasions during the war. Therefore a case can be made out for having a number of bases in the Middle East with sufficient strength in land and air forces, not to absorb the initial shock of a major attack, but to carry out what are politely known as 'police duties'.

In practice, of course, the strategic argument in favour of retaining the western position in the Middle East is a combination of all these points. Later in this essay I shall try to test the validity of the argument in general.

The interest in oil is newer, dating only from the beginning of this century, but it is complicated by the constant process of change which the industry is undergoing as production expands, royalty payments increase, and as new fields or rumours of fields are found in areas whose political status is not always clear. Furthermore, whereas in the strategic aspects of their policy, Britain and America are on more or less common ground, they are in open competition when it comes to oil. That is one of the reasons (though by no means the only one) why Britain tries with such pathetic earnestness to follow a 'British' as distinct from a western policy in relation to the Middle East. Exclusive control of certain of the oilfields is inextricably bound up with current conceptions of 'British prestige', and both the Foreign Office and the State Department have allowed themselves to slip into the absurd position where the actions they take in support of their oil *protégés* are in open contradiction of their policy of military alliances—the ultimate absurdity being that an American company pays large sums to Saudi Arabia, which uses them to finance nationalist movements against America's chief ally. But that is anticipating a later part of the argument.

The first successful oil-wells in the Middle East were sunk in the Khuzistan district of Persia in 1908. Except for some in Egypt, no other oil was actually found in exploitable form before the first World War, though enormous quantities existed in the hopes of prospectors and the holders of concessions enthusiastically taken up from the Ottoman government, and a major international company, the Turkish Petroleum Company, was set up in 1911. At Versailles oil was constantly present in the background, but it played a remarkably small part in determining the pattern of the Middle Eastern settlement. The Mosul area, where pre-war hopes were highest, was actually allocated to France by the Sykes-Picot agreement, and transferred to Britain only by a separate agreement between Lloyd George and Clemenceau in December 1918; in return, France received the former German shareholding in the Turkish Petroleum Company and a right to a quarter of the oil extracted, on condition that she built a pipeline across Syria to the Mediterranean.

The first big oil strike in Iraq was not at Mosul, but at Kirkuk in 1927. In the next two decades several other fields were brought into production—Bahrein in 1934, Saudi Arabia in 1939, Kuwait in 1946 and Qatar in 1949. Until 1950, the year before the Abadan crisis, Persia was still the largest producing country, but would have been overtaken by Saudi Arabia in 1951, and probably by Kuwait in 1952, even if the wells had not gone out of production. In 1955 the combined output of the six producing countries was 158 million tons of crude oil, or 21.5 per cent of the total for the world. (The details were: Kuwait 54.8 million tons, Saudi Arabia 47.1, Iraq 33.2, Persia 16.0, Qatar 5.4 and Bahrein 1.5; Persian production was still not fully back to normal, but was to increase in subsequent years by agreement with the Consortium.) Other oilfields were known or believed to exist in Oman—hence the curious episode in December 1955 when the Sultan of Oman, with British support, drove out a rebellious Imam backed by Saudi Arabia—and possibly in the Yemen as well.

Apart from the fact that the Persian Gulf area is the second largest producer of oil in the world, and the chief source of supply to Britain and western Europe, western capital is also heavily committed in the industry; the crux of the Abadan dispute was less the loss of oil production than the threat Dr. Mosadeq presented to the security of western investments. This is also the principal reason why the countries lucky enough to possess oil are in so strong a bargaining position in dealing with the western countries, for it needs only a hint of another Abadan to compel the companies to agree to higher royalty payments to the local governments. Apart from the protectorates (Kuwait, Bahrein and Qatar) the oil countries are fully independent at least in principle, and it has become a major western interest to see that they are controlled by governments not likely to repeat the actions of Dr. Mossadeq. On a number of occasions western intervention has forced refractory governments out in favour of something more amenable—though it stays on the record that two such attempts in Persia, in 1933 and 1950, failed and recoiled on the heads of the oil companies.

If one adds to the threat of expropriation the risk that an anti-western government in an oil country may also be a pro-Soviet one, a picture builds up so alarming as to justify, at first impression, almost any sort of policy which will avert the danger. The threat that the Soviet Union may come to control the oilfields is, in essence, the same as the threat that she may gain direct access to the Persian Gulf, and the necessary counter-policies are the same in either case. But both are cases where the first impression is likely to be the wrong one. To identify anti-western nationalism with Soviet influence is as grave a mistake as can be made. It may indeed be necessary eventually to come to terms with the nationalists in order to *prevent* the Soviet Union from gaining control, and to sacrifice a part of the western interest in order to keep the rest—to agree, in fact, to a radical revision of the oil relationships in order to avoid driving the nationalist movements into communist hands. That unfortunately, is a difficult idea to explain to people who are determined to take the short view.

II

STRATEGY, in its broadest meaning, and oil are thus the principal reasons why the west is interested in the Middle East; there are others, such as the quantities of western capital invested in merchanting and other activities, but these are of lesser importance.

The countries in which these interests are situated have it in common that all of them except Persia were once part of the Ottoman Empire, all except Israel and Persia are Arabic-speaking or mainly so, and all except Israel and Lebanon are Moslem by religion and more or less feudal in their social structure. Be-

fore the first World War Persia had already made some impact
on international affairs, having originally been supported by
Britain as a bulwark against Russian encroachment to the south
and then divided by the Anglo-Russian treaty of 1907 into two
spheres of influence—a division which distinctly annoyed the
Persian nationalists. Egypt was virtually independent of the
Porte from the time of Mehemet Ali, and in later years was
under a sort of British tutelage which became a formal protectorate from 1914 till Saad Zaghlul forced its end in 1922. In the
Arabian peninsula the control of the Porte was shadowy; Aden
was a British colony and the surrounding area a protectorate,
and British power was established among the shiekdoms of the
Persian Gulf, while in the rest of the peninsula local tribal chiefs
were the real rulers. In the Levant there were considerable French
commercial interests (as there were in Egypt), and France claim-
ed the right of succession in the event of the collapse of the
Empire. But the Levant and the lower Tigris-Euphrates valley
—the modern Iraq—were under effective control from Constantinople, and in 1914 it was still premature to talk about
rights of succession.

When the war ended there was no more Ottoman Empire,
and Russia and Germany were no longer in a position to take
part in the settlement of the Eastern Question. Britain and
France were accordingly able to play out a happy little diplomatic game between themselves, with such attention as they
thought fit to the long list of promises and counter-promises
made to various people during the war. The first set, the exchange of letters between Sir Henry McMahon and the Sherif
Hussein of Mecca, pledged Britain to support the creation of an
Arab kingdom with rather uncertain boundaries, but definitely
excluding most of the Mediterranean seaboard and the lower
part of Mesopotamia. The second, the Sykes-Picot agreement,
drew a theoretical line from the Red Sea to the Persian Gulf;
the quadrilateral formed by this line on the south, the Persian
frontier on the east, the Taurus on the north and the Mediterranean on the west was to be divided into British and French
spheres of influence, while Russia was to get territory further
north. The agreement referred specifically to the obligation of
France and Britain to 'recognise and uphold an independent

Arab state or a Confederation of Arab states' in the areas not directly annexed—that is, in roughly the same areas as the kingdom proposed in the Hussein-McMahon letters—but said nothing about what sort of state this was to be. The third document was, of course, the Balfour Declaration of December 1917, with its imprecise promise of a national home for the Jews in Palestine.

The Arab Kingdom never materialised, partly because of jealousies in the Hashemi family who were to supply its ruler, but even more because neither Britain nor France sufficiently trusted the other to stick to the spirit of the Sykes-Picot agreement and not to try to convert the spheres of influence into areas of direct control. Consequently the curious institution of the Class A mandate was invented specially to fit the circumstances of the quadrilateral, and in place of a unitary Arab Kingdom no fewer than five new states were created and placed under mandate—Syria and Lebanon to France, and Iraq, Transjordan and Palestine to Britain. A case could be made out for excluding Palestine because of the Balfour Declaration, and possibly also the Lebanon because of its large Christian population. But the other three deserved no such special treatment, since they were divided by no natural frontier of geography, history, race, religion or language. They remain as monuments to Anglo-French jealousy, and once their creation was decided upon all that was needed was for the mandatory powers to infect them with the characteristically European disease of nationalism and to play on the nationalist feeling which then arose as a means of keeping them apart, and so under effective western dominance.

The other principal characteristics of the Arab states and Persia are their low level of development, the poverty of the mass of their peoples contrasting with the ostentatious wealth of the upper classes, and their unwillingness to absorb the ideals of parliamentary democracy which were once supposed to be among the west's most valuable exports. All the northern Arab countries have experimented with democracy, and so has Persia, but the only one where the experiment has been anything like successful is the Lebanon. The southern countries have never even tried it. Democracy does, as a matter of fact, have some grave disadvantages for countries placed as most of these are, for when the main object of policy is to get rid of outside control, negotiation by elected governments seldom works as well or as quickly as the more ruthless methods of dictators. That is why nationalist movements so easily become authoritarian. In the Middle East the classic case is Egypt, where Saad Zaghlul found that it was no use setting up a nationalist political party if it was to work only by constitutional means, and where more recently the dictatorial Neguib-Nasser régime achieved with comparative ease what Mustafa el-Nahas and the other parliamentary leaders had failed to get after years of bargaining.

But in any case democracy and extreme poverty do not go well together. The standard of living of the peasant in any country from Egypt to Persia is little above the subsistence level, and cannot be greatly improved without a complete recasting of the systems of land tenure, vast expenditure on irrigation and the control of erosion, the bringing of new techniques to the land, and in most countries the extension of industrialisation too as a means of reducing agrarian overpopulation. Even the highly developed agriculture of the Nile delta does not make the peasants wealthy; the delta is grossly overcrowded, and in spite of Nasser's reforms a high proportion of what the land produces never becomes the property of the peasant at all. In Jordan and Syria potentially rich wheat lands suffer from lack of water, primitive methods of cultivation, unsuitable seed and all the other marks of a backward agriculture. In Iraq millions of acres between the rivers and in their lower courses which used to be one of the richest agrarian regions of the world have gone out of cultivation altogether, so that the population of the valleys is now smaller than it was in the time of the Caliphate; the Iraq Development Board is gradually changing the picture, but it will be years before the former position can be restored. Only in the well-watered valleys of the Lebanon do the yield of most crops come anywhere near European levels.

Although Cairo, Damascus, Baghdad and Teheran are in their way wealthy places, the lasting impression one retains of any of them is one of grinding poverty surrounding a small, prosperous centre where wealthy European standards prevail. The towns carry considerably larger populations than their industries would warrant, since they are a refuge for thousands of peasants who cannot make a living on the land. The remarkable

thing about them is that they breed comparatively small communist movements; even the ill-paid small officials, schoolmas-
ters and letter-writers who form the intelligentsia of the slums,
and whose sense of social frustration might be expected to lead
them into communism, tend rather more to Moslem orthodoxy
and extremism of the right, like the now forbidden Moslem
Brotherhood in Egypt.

The situation in the oil countries is hardly any better than in
the others, even though the revenues received from oil are now
running at some £360 million a year and are likely to increase
still further. While the companies have built model villages
with amenities approaching the European in the immediate
neighbourhood of the oilfields, areas without oil have not bene-
fited, and their resentment is increased rather than diminsihed
when the show-places of Abadan or Kirkuk are held up to them
to prove how well-disposed the companies really are. Although
the oil revenues are a main source of state finance for all the oil
countries, and practically the only source for one or two, it is
easy for a nationalist to hold up the continuance of extensive
foreign interests as the cause of the poverty from which most of
the country suffers; that is why Dr. Mossadeq and the Tudeh
found the forging of their unholy alliance so simple a task, and
why from one end of the Middle East to the other popular support can often by engineered for the most feudally-minded of
political systems.

It is not quite correct to say that the terms 'right' and 'left' are
meaningless in the political pattern of the Arab countries, but
they do not mean anything like the same as in western Europe.
In the absence of popular reforming movements with mass support, almost any piece of reform so far carried through has been
the work of men who cannot be regarded as 'left' in the European sense. Kemal Atatürk in Turkey was a dictator who relied
on strong-arm methods, often of questionable morality, yet he
was the outstanding reformer of the modern Moslem world.
Riza Shah Pahlevi in Persia was also a reformer, yet his rule,
always dictatorial, degenerated in the end into a pure oriental
despotism. Nasser in Egypt, and the unsuccessful Shishakly in
Syria, are examples of others who threw overboard any pretence at democracy in order to modify the archaic social struc-

ture of their countries, and the so-called 'democratic' opposition
to them usually wanted to return to old systems in which the
landowner and the merchant could recover their former pre-
eminent positions at the expense of the peasant and the town
worker. 'Socialist' parties, where they exist, are mainly middle
class groups (possibly favouring the merchants against the landowners, but sometimes not even going as far as that) and are far
removed in outlook from the social-democrats of Europe. With
the possible exception of the Lebanon, where the socialist party
is more or less recognisable by western standards, no Arab country has yet thrown up a popular, democratic reformist movement, and none is likely to do so in the foreseeable future; if
reform is to come from within, it is much more likely to be
through the means of 'progressive despotisms' such as are occa-
sionally produced in countries at a certain stage in the process of
development from the primitive to the modern—a stage which
all the Middle Eastern countries except Saudi Arabia, the Yemen
and some of the sheikdoms have either reached or are nearing.
But one of the major facts in Middle Eastern politics, and one
which the western countries will ignore at their peril, is that
these 'progressive despotisms' will owe a large part of their support to their ability in reducing or eliminating western influence
in their countries. For though the alliance between Mossadeq
and the Tudeh may have been an unholy one, there was considerable force in the arguments on which it rested. In the next
stage of development a combination against foreign influence of
all sorts of forces is by no means unlikely. Apparently right-
wing nationalism and apparently left-wing reformism are not
unnatural allies in the Middle Eastern setting.

III

BETWEEN 1940 and 1945 there was perhaps an opportunity to
undo some of the harm that had been done at Versailles, but it
was not taken. Once the recalcitrants Dentz in Syria, Rashid
Ali el-Gailani in Iraq, Riza Shah Pahlevi in Persia and the Mufti
of Jerusalem in Palestine had been got rid of, a sort of organic
unity was imposed on the whole of the Middle East; Palestine
was the only obvious discordant note, and few people had begun to appreciate that the newly-acquired American interest in

Arabian oil was going to prove a second one. In 1941 the British Government set up the Middle East Supply Centre to coordinate the civilian needs of the area and to reconcile them with the limited shipping available; later the Americans came into the organisation as well. Until the late summer of 1944 the Centre acted as a control on virtually all imports into the Middle East, which gave it a powerful weapon of wider economic control, for since most imports had to be carried in ships owned or regulated by the major allies, the Middle Eastern governments had to accept the Centre or else go without. What few people realised at first (though it dawned on them later) was that the MESC was a fascinating experiment in large-scale regional economic planning, and long before its demise it was doing many things which had no more than a tenuous connection with the control of imports. The British and American officials who ran it were inevitably accused of 'empire-building'—not an uncommon charge, and frequently not an unjustified one, in the hectic and jealousy-ridden atmosphere of wartime Cairo—and had to face constant criticism from people in responsible positions who did not grasp what was really going on. Once the war had been taken outside the area and conditions began to return to 'normal', the pressures for restoring the old merchants increased, and the first serious rift in the unity of the western approach appeared when the American element became suspicious that the whole organisation was nothing more than a sinister British plot to retain effective imperial control when the war was over. So in the spring of 1945 the Centre was wound up, and with it there passed the best opportunity since 1918 to induce the fragmented Arab world to cooperate on the economic if not the political plane.

On the political level too there were tentative moves in the direction of unity. Nuri es-Said, Prime Minister of Iraq with British support after the expulsion of Rashid Ali, was openly and sincerely pan-Arab in outlook, and in 1943 had suggested the union of Syria, Lebanaon, Transjordan and Palestine into a single state with close ties of alliance with Iraq. Even earlier the British Government had hinted at support for 'any scheme that commands general approval' for bringing the Arab countries closer together,* and as the war drew to its end, Britain was commonly believed throughout the Middle East to favour a Greater Syria under one branch or other of the Hashemi family. Whatever the reason, all these tentative ideas were dropped, and in the end the one piece of political coordination left behind by the war was the dubious machinery of the Arab League, set up with British blessing in March 1945. One need not go into all the complicated history of the League and the extent to which it was made or marred by Egypt's bid for the leadership of the Moslem world (it was once suggested, for instance, that the Caliphate should be revived in the person of King Farouk); the essential point about it is that it never became an effective organism of Arab unity. Indeed, the only major piece of coordination it attempted was during the Palestine war of 1948, and it did not do that particularly well.

The events of 1948 were, in their way, as decisive for the pattern of Middle Eastern relationships as were those of 1919. Following the Arab rising in Palestine in 1937, the situation there was kept more or less quiet during the war by military occupation and the restrictions of Jewish immigration in accordance with the 1939 White Paper; but since there were no clear indications of what sort of policy was to follow the White Paper, the temptation for the Jews to increase their pressure on the British in the later days of the war became irresistible, and by the spring of 1944 violence had begun once again. The choice for Britain, as mandatory, was not whether to allow a Jewish state or not, but whether it was to come into being by peaceful or by violent means, and because the Labour Government immediately after 1945 did not face the issue squarely and decide on a policy it must bear a share of the responsbiility for the tragedy. The pressures on the Foreign Office and the American State Department were enormous and in contradictory directions. Yet when one recalls how long a warning was given of the need for decision, one cannot fail to be surprised at the complete absence of a coherent policy when the moment actually arrived.

By 1947, when the British Government announced its inten-

*Eden at the Mansion House, 29th May, 1941

tion to surrender the mandate, there could be no question that
the term 'national home' as used in the Balfour Declaration
meant anything but a Jewish state. It is completely pointless
now to argue whether that did or did not run counter to Mc-
Mahon's undertakings to the Sherif Hussein in 1916; the important point is that a Jewish state could not be created without
doing violence to Arab feelings and Arab rights. But it was impossible not to create a Jewish state without doing equal violence
to Jewish feelings and to the spirit of promises made in the past.
The report of the Anglo-American Commission of Inquiry in
1947, like the later United Nations resolution, was an attempt
to reconcile what could not really be reconciled. Both bitterly
offended the Arabs without satisfying the Jews. But it was Arab
disunity and jealousy, together with poor leadership from
Egypt, which determined the outcome; the Arab governments
rejected the United Nations resolution but proved incapable of
getting a more satisfactory settlement by force. The fact that the
Arab League had failed at its first big test increased the mutual
jealousies of its members and drove Egypt into a sort of dis-
graced isolation for a time. So lacking was any real spirit of
unity among the Arab countries that none—not even the wealthy recipients of oil revenues—were willing to give effective aid
to Jordan in the herculean task of digesting 800,000 refugees.

Among the many lessons which can be drawn from this sad
piece of history two are of particular importance. It was the first
occasion on which the United Nations tried to bring about a
territorial change by peaceful means, and found it an extremely
difficult operation. It was not the sort of dispute that could have
been settled by judicial methods, since none of the various documents produced was really very relevant to the conditions of
1948, and all of them could be dismissed on the ground that
they were not treaties between states, but merely promises made
by governments to individuals and organisms which were, at
the time the promises were made, entirely unofficial. The only
basis on which the issue could be decided was one of equity. But
equity is a concept which does not stand up well to discussion
in a body like the Security Council or the General Assembly,
where none of those sitting in judgment are entirely free from
interest. Nor is it easy to find a basis in equity for a change

which inevitably deprives certain people of rights to which they can prove a reasonably good title, as the Palestine Arabs certainly could to the lands which they and their ancestors had owned for generations. Yet, in the circumstances, there was an overwhelming moral responsibility on the rest of the world, and in Britain in particular, to see that the state of Israel was created.

Like the case of Viet Nam six years later, the way in which it was done raised doubts as to whether an international body is ever likely to sponsor change by peaceful means and see that its decisions are carried through. What brought Israel into existence was, in the end, not an agreed decision but the force of arms, and all that the United Nations was able to do afterwards was to take note of the fact and try to prevent any further change from being made by similar methods. The implication is a very far-reaching one—that a collective security organisation is bound by its very nature to favour the *status quo*, while the initiative for change comes not from agreement but from force. But to argue that out to its full extent would go far outside the limits of an essay on the Middle East.

The second principal lesson is that no government should ever let itself be landed in the position of Britain while the dispute was at its height. Compelled by the course of events to accept the creation of Israel, but anxious at the same time not to offend the Arabs, the British government fell between the two stools, losing Arab confidence without at first gaining that of Israel. Once the fact of Israel was accepted, it was necessary for Britain (and for the American Administration) to make it clear beyond all possible doubt that the new state would be protected, and even the 1950 declaration did not do this in sufficiently unequivocal terms. A great deal of the trouble which has occurred in the Middle East since 1948 arises from the absence of certainty that Britain and America really do recognise Israel's territorial integrity and are not prepared to trade, for instance, the Negev for some sort of concession from the Arab countries. This absence of certainty is one of the reasons why no Arab state has yet recognised Israel—and why, eight years after the event, the wretched refugees are still crowded in camps instead of being settled on lands which they can regard as a new but permanent

home. Why, after all, should the Arab countries end the state of
war which endows them with so useful a bargaining counter?

IV

THE year 1954 was one in which several stories came to their
end, and few people realised that a new and more critical phase
of history was on the point of beginning. The Arab-Israel dispute was no nearer a settlement, but it was tolerably quiescent;
a few frontier incidents reminded people of its existence, and
Egypt still imposed a blockade of the Gulf of Aqaba, but on the
whole things were so quiet that talk of a possible settlement
began now and then to be heard. In Persia Dr. Mossadeq and
his erratic régime had been swept away, a new oil agreement
had been negotiated, and Abadan was beginning to regain something of its former activity. In Egypt, two years after the revolution, the greatest success of all had been secured with the
agreement under which the British were to evacuate the Canal
zone. In Iraq, it passed almost unnoticed by the rest of the world
when parliamentary government broke down, and the inevitable Nuri es-Said returned to power once again, this time as all
but a dictator. The other oil countries in the south produced
ever larger quantities of oil, while rumours began to be heard of
possible huge new deposits in parts of the Arab world hitherto
hardly explored. Apart from the ever-present problem of Israel,
the only jarring note in this harmonious picture was towards the
end of the year when orthodox Moslems in Syria demonstrated
against the Egyptian government for its suppression of the Moslem Brotherhood, and an awkward dispute arose between the
two countries. But within a few months that dispute was to
seem ludicrously irrelevant to the real points at issue in the Middle East, and Egypt and Syria were forced together in dramatic
style.

The initiative for the Baghdad Pact of February 1955 came
from the American State Department. Something of the sort
was in line with other American diplomatic activities; Turkey
was already guaranteed under the Truman Doctrine, Pakistan
had accepted military aid even at the cost of exacerbating her
relations with India, and no doubt it seemed logical enough to
try to complete the 'northern tier' by bringing the two together

with Iraq and Persia and anyone else who would come in. It seems that neither the State Department nor the British Foreign Office anticipated the effect on Egypt of a treaty of this sort signed between Iraq, a member of the Arab League, and Turkey, the non-Arab Moslem power for whom Egypt's jealousy was specially reserved. The immediate reaction was one of suspicion both that Turkey was now making a bid for the leadership in the Middle East which she had lost after the first World War, and that Britain, and less directly the United States, were hoping to use the Baghdad Pact to restore their vanishing control over the Arab world and were using Turkey as a tool to give the operation an aura of respectability. The American hand in the Baghdad Pact seems not to have been noticed at first; of the non-Moslem countries concerned, Britain received the greatest share of the odium, doubtless because the pact looked like a sort of compensation for the lost base in the Canal zone—as indeed it was partly intended to be.

The British attitude was capable of a number of interpretations, and the true one is probably something of a mixture. When the original pact was signed between Turkey and Iraq in February 1955 it was presented as open to the accession of any country recognised by both the original signatories (a formula designed to exclude Israel, which was not recognised by Iraq); and when four countries had joined a permanent organisation was to be set up to coordinate not only defence but also economic policies in the field of development. Britain became the third member of the pact, and when first Persia and then Pakistan joined in September 1955 the way was open to establish the permanent organisation; this was done at a conference in Baghdad in November with full British participation, though the more cautious Americans only sent sympathetic observers. Behind this British enthusiasm there was, first, the argument that the pact would actually do something to make up for the Suez base; secondly, the belief that a joint military-economic organisation might now succeed where previous efforts to create Arab unity had failed; and thirdly, the hardly-formulated hope that if a number of Arab countries could be brought together on a basis of self-interest with Turkey and others, they might even be induced in time to recognise Israel. There were, unfortunately, a number of fallacies in this whole conception, and in practically every respect the performance of the pact fell far short of what had been hoped from it.

Egypt apart, the whole scheme betrays a considerable miscalculation of the mood of the other Arab countries. None of its sponsors can seriously have expected Egypt to join, but they certainly did expect to bring in Syria, Lebanon and Jordan, and it was a shock when Syria (under a new government) composed her differences with Egypt and followed the Cairo lead against the pact. With Syria out, there could be little hope of getting the Lebanon to come in, and Jordan, the weakest and most financially dependent of the Levant states, was anxious to assert what independence she could and to associate herself with the Syrian attitude. In particular the suspicion (whether justified or not no longer matters) that the price of joining would be the recognition of Israel so alarmed the more intransigent elements in all three countries that no government would have dared to risk offending them—which is why, at the end of 1955, a curiously heavy-handed British approach to Jordan led not to her joining the pact but to the forcible overthrow of the government that had conducted the negotiations, and then to the abrupt dismissal of the British commander of the Arab Legion.

The immediate result of the pact was the virtual demise of the Arab League and a rapid effort by Egypt to secure a new alignment of the anti-pact countries—Saudi Arabia and Syria especially. The less immediate, but no less direct, consequence was that Egypt began to put out feelers for a more powerful backer against the attempt of the western powers to organise the 'northern tier', and from this the purchase of arms from a country in the communist bloc followed perfectly logically. It all suited the Soviet book remarkably well, and as I said at the beginning of this essay the only surprising thing about this re-entry of Russia into the Eastern Question was that it had not taken place much earlier.

It would be quite wrong to condemn the Baghdad Pact merely because it provoked counter-action by the Soviet Union; governments cannot, in international politics any more than in home affairs, refrain from action merely because someone else may not like it. Nor does the pact stand condemned simply because its effects were miscalculated; the only blame for that attaches to the people who misinformed the Government, or to the Government itself if the right advice was offered and not taken. As a matter of fact, it would be wrong to condemn the pact in all its aspects, for especially after the conference at Baghdad in November 1955, it began to look as though it might contain some elements of common sense, particularly in so far as it made provision for coordinated economic action between the signatories—but that is not to say that both its handling and some of the political and military assumptions behind it are not open to serious criticism.

The first line of criticism brings us back to the discussion of the strategic role of the Middle East. Presumably no one will claim that any form of military arrangement based on the 'northern tier' (or even more widely based) is likely to guarantee the region against being attacked or overrun in the event of a major war. If a major war does take place, it will be because of decisions taken far from the Arab world, and it would require vastly more force than can at present be disposed of in the area to defend it against a full-scale military assault from the north—let alone destruction with nuclear weapons. So if a case is to be made out for any sort of military agreement with any or all of the Arab countries, it must rest on one or more of the other three arguments—that it will deny the Russians access *in peacetime* to the oilfields and the ports on the Indian Ocean, that it will preserve for western use in case of need a jumping-off ground against the Soviet Union, or that it will help to ensure stability in the area and give the west the opportunity to deal with local disturbances before they become serious. Any one of the three arguments must assume that at least one western base is kept somewhere in the region—in Cyprus, at Dhahran or elsewhere.

Yet are these arguments beyond question? There is every reason why the west should want the Middle East to be stable, since the economic stake there is enormous, and would still be even if all the oil countries were to expropriate all the oil companies. But the prime need is for political rather than military stability —a difficult concept, but one which needs to be thought out with the greatest care—and the whole validity of the military argument depends on whether action to secure military stability increases or decreases political stability. If the effect of a military pact is to split the Arab countries into opposing blocs and drag them into the main east-west alignments, it will have decreased stability; the military cart will have been put before the political horse. To anyone writing in the early part of 1956 it looks as if that is precisely what has happened. In the seven years of cold war up to 1955, the Arab world stood almost entirely outside it, engaged in its own disputes and preoccupied with its own difficulties, none of which had much to do with the wider troubles of the world. When I say that the mere fact that the Soviet Union did not like the Baghdad Pact was not enough to condemn it, that is not to suggest that the Foreign Office and the State Department should not have anticipated that this very natural Soviet reaction would have the effect of extending the cold war to the Middle East, even at a time when it was relaxing in almost all its other theatres. If they did anticipate that and still went ahead with the military side of the pact, they were guilty of criminal folly in staking the certainty of grave political disadvantage against a wholly problematic military advantage.

The second line of criticism concerns the handling rather than the concept of the pact. It was a mistake of the first order for Britain to become a full member of the organisation set up under it. Even a military agreement between the northern tier countries alone would have been considerably less objectionable, since the member countries would at least have been able to avoid the odium of openly committing themselves to the western bloc. If the eventual emphasis is to be placed on the economic side of the organisation, it would still be far better for Britain and the other western powers to be less directly associated —a point on which the Americans were wiser than the British, since they declined to join the pact in the full sense although they were willing to show a friendly interest, in the knowledge that the financial assistance needed to make a reality of economic development would have to come mainly from western sources anyway.

The third objection is that nothing in the pact helped to settle the chief current political problem of the Middle East itself, which is still the question of Isreal. It may be that both western

governments hoped that the original pact between Turkey and
Iraq would induce Iraq to recognise Israel's existence; Iraq has
no common frontier with Israel, was of all the Arab countries
the least involved in the war of 1948, and the most likely to take
the initiative for a settlement, and something would have been
gained if only one Arab state had been induced to take the
plunge. But if the hope was there the ground was extraordinarily badly prepared. For in the early part of 1955 there was not
the slightest chance that any country except Iraq would be persuaded in favour of recognition, and the mere suggestion was
enough to make the other Arab governments bristle. Yet even
Iraq could not be expected to run so far foul of her Arab neighbours unless it was perfectly clear that Israel was a permanent
fact backed by the determination of the western powers—and
that, unfortunately, western policy had miserably failed to make
clear.

V

WHAT, then, ought a long-term western policy towards the
Middle East to be? It is much easier to say what it ought not to
be. It ought not to rest too heavily on military arrangements,
and might even be better without them altogether. It ought not
to assume the indefinite continuance of western control, however indirect, in those areas where control is still maintained. It
ought not to count on there always being men like Nuri es-Said
to help out at awkward junctures, but should be far more prepared for Neguibs and Nassers, perhaps even for Mossadeqs.

One of the essential prerequisites to a long term policy is that
the western countries should make clear beyond any possible
doubt what their policy towards Isreal really is. A large part of
the resentment felt by the Arab states is due to the belief that
Israel is a western creation and an outpost of western influence,
as indeed, in some respects, she is. But there can now be no
question of going back on the decision taken in 1948 by which
this new political element was introduced into the Middle Eastern scene. But uncertainty about the western attitude stimulates
the Arab governments to hope that concessions can be wrung
by the simple expedient of always asking for more than they
really expect to get, and until the west defines the precise extent

to which it will support Israel against Arab demands there will
be no stability on her borders. By the same token, this uncertainty also encourages the more intransigent elements inside
Israel—the advocates of a preventive war who in March 1956
actually took their proposals to the floor of the Knesset and
showed that they could call upon a disconcertingly large measure of support—and so provide still further fuel for Arab distrust and hostility.

There is no value in statements, however often reiterated, that
the west will guarantee 'agreed' frontiers, since there is not the
slightest likelihood that Israel and the Arabs will be able to agree
on modifications of the armistice line unless they know that the
west is prepared to guarantee something very much like the
armistice line itself; minor adjustments may be possible, but in
the present atmosphere major changes (such as the exchange of
the southern Negev for the Gaza strip, as has sometimes been
suggested) cannot be put forward with any hope of success.
That is why Sir Anthony Eden's Guildhall speech in November
1955 was so completely wide of the mark, for to suggest the
possibility of major changes is to encourage intransigence on
both sides, to diminish stability rather than to create it. A guarantee must be given (if possible with Soviet agreement, otherwise without it, though the Soviet declaration of April 1956
suggests that agreement might be possible) to protect Israel from
Arab incursions and the Arab countries from a preventive war
by Israel, and must be accompanied by clear and decisive action
to maintain a balance in the armed strength of the two sides
while avoiding competitive arming. Once given, the guarantee
ought to become as essential an ingredient of western policy as
the Truman Doctrine in relation to Greece and Turkey or the
38th parallel in Korea.

A second prerequisite is that western policy towards the Middle East must be agreed between the British and American governments. Ever since the American oil interest in Saudi Arabia
became big enough to challenge the older British interests in
Persia and Iraq, there has been a tendency for the two governments to act as though they could follow individual policies, to
the irritation of their friends and the amusement of their enemies; and matters have been made worse still by open disagree-

ments between Britain and America on one side and France on the other. One might instance, as an example of the first fault in western diplomacy, America's sensitivity to any criticism of Saudi Arabia even at a time when that government was sponsoring action against the Baghdad Pact (after all, an American invention) and against British influence generally. Similarly, the Buraimi and Oman disputes of 1955 were known by everyone to be, in their essence, conflicts between oil interests supported by the two western governments. The clearest case of the second fault has been France's attitude to the Baghdad Pact and the failure of both France and the other western governments to grasp that there is a close connection between what happens in Egypt, the Persian Gulf or the Levant and the evolution of French policy in the Moslem countries of North Africa. (The main inconsistency here was a French one. M. Pineau's criticism of the Baghdad Pact was very much on the same grounds as my own, but did not tie in with his efforts to secure support for a dubious policy in North Africa; the British and Americans may have been wrong on both counts, but at least they were consistently wrong).

Such failures of coordination simply encourage the belief, now widespread in the Arab world, that there is something to be gained by playing off the western countries against each other, and all of them against the Russians. Yet when Sir Anthony Eden went to Washington early in 1956 he brought back with him no assurance that any serious effort had been made to find a way out of the difficulty. In the months that followed there were constant rumours that Britain was reappraising her policy with a view to going it alone rather than seeking closer coordination—rumours which bore out the known resentment of the British Foreign Office at the irruption of the Americans into a field of politics in which, in spite of the long succession of disasters, British diplomats still claim to have a particular *expertise*.

I want, in the closing section of this essay, to outline what I believe to be the essential lines of a long term policy. This policy will mean the jettisoning of many old ideas and habits, and for that reason alone it is absolutely necessary that there should be agreement between the western powers on what they are aiming to do. There is no scope in it for the no doubt brilliant but erratic and often irresponsible figures of the old diplomacy in the Middle East—the men who landed Britain, after 1918, with a host of irreconcilable promises or who, after 1945, retained such confidence in their skill in bargaining with individual Arab leaders that they caused British policy to follow a course which can only be described as tortuous. All three western governments, having once agreed their policy, must be prepared to follow it out with the greatest possible consistency and with the closest control over those who have to execute it on the spot. They must realise, too, that the time is now gone when they can safely try to move Arab governments about like pieces on a chessboard, playing off one against another in a manner which may once have been possible, but which the west no longer has sufficient authority to do successfully even it it were desirable.

The penultimate aim must be to draw the Arab countries together in joint action to tackle the appalling economic problems of the area; the ultimate aim will be to bring in Israel as well. There are so many points of economic and social structure in common between the Middle Eastern countries, and the frontiers between them are so artificial, that only a joint approach is likely to find solutions to their difficulties. Precedents are dangerous things to quote, but one of the best things that could be done now is for all the governments concerned to recall the successes of the Middle East Supply Centre in its limited field and to examine the possibilities of extending the same sort of organisation to cover a wider range of activities; the tragedy is that the political cooperation which made the Centre possible during the war has been allowed to evaporate since. But it is essential to restore it.

The one sound element of the Baghdad Pact was that it provided for joint economic action between the signatory countries; its supreme error was that it made the benefits of such action conditional on accepting a military commitment which the great majority of the Arab world does not want. People in the west must realise that the Arab governments need external assistance but see no reason why they should accept it from the west any more than from the Soviet Union or anyone else prepared to offer it to them. They are in a strong bargaining position, and know it. If the west attempts to lay down too strict

conditions for the giving of economic aid, all that will happen
is that the Middle Eastern countries will turn elsewhere, and the
Soviet Union will be encouraged to make further offers on the
lines already indicated when, for instance, she proposed financial
assistance for the High Dam project in Egypt, for more general
aid to Saudi Arabia, or in March 1956 to Pakistan.

Why, someone in the west may ask, should aid be given
without anything in return in the shape of a military or political
commitment? The question is a natural one, but all the same is
based on a misunderstanding of the Middle Eastern situation.
Even from a narrowly western point of view, the essential is
that the aid should be available, since it is the only way to create
the economic stability which is the west's primary concern in
the area, and if it does not come from the west it will come from
somewhere else. Where the aid comes from is less important
even from a western point of view than that it should come, and
in adequate quantity. The west should therefore try to ensure
that aid from all sources is enough, rather than to embark on a
process of competitive bidding for exclusive support.

This, then, implies that whatever form of joint economic organisation eventually emerges there must be no discrimination
between the receiving countries according to whether they accept a military commitment or not. There is no reason why the
principle of non-discrimination should be any more difficult to
apply in a Middle Eastern context than it was under the Colombo Plan in southern Asia or under the original form of the Marshall Plan in Europe before the Soviet Union rejected the American offer. There are even precedents in the Middle East itself,
since some of the existing plans for aid for specific projects (for
instance, the Johnston plan for the development of the Jordan,
or the contributions of the World Bank to the Iraq Development Board) are free from political and military strings; they
are indeed well conceived, and all that is wrong with them is
that they are on too limited a scale as yet.

The Marshall Plan is perhaps the best model to follow, since
it included the two important elements of external aid and mutual cooperation. If the Soviet Union can be induced to take
part in a general scheme, so much the better; if not, it is still
surely worth while for the western countries, to go ahead in the

knowledge that political and economic stability in so critical a part of the world is worth paying for.

This leads to another and no less important point. Up to the moment, there has been no serious trouble in any of the oil countries except Persia, but there can be no guarantee that this placid state of affairs will continue indefinitely; indeed, all the indications are that if the west tries to assert its influence by tying down 'reliable' governments such as that of Nuri es-Said, the nationalist reaction that such behaviour is apt to provoke will turn against the oil interests as well. There are two distinct problems. The first is whether the oil companies are justified in continuing to withdraw from the oil areas as large a proportion of the profits as they do; the second concerns the disposal of the £360 million left in the area in accordance with the various agreements between the companies and the governments. There is a case for suggesting that the companies should leave behind in the producing countries a larger share of the profits than they do at present, but I do not believe that such a case can be established so long as the present type of agreement lasts. An increase in the oil royalties now would simply mean that even more money would go to the wrong people.

Most of the agreements do, in fact, provide that a proportion of the oil revenues received by the governments should be used for economic development, and in the particular case of Iraq as much as 70 per cent is paid over to furnish a large part of the income of the Iraq Development Board. In Kuwait they account for almost the whole revenue of the state, and work out at something over £500 per year for every man, woman and child in the country. In Kuwait, Bahrein, Qatar and Saudi Arabia the chief result of these enormous payments is to make the small wealthy class wealthier still. It is surely an absurdity that in an area where economic development is so much a matter of urgency, something like £360 million should have been paid over in 1955 with so little effective control over its use, and with no provision at all that any part of the revenues should help the countries which are not lucky enough to possess oil in exploitable quantities. Ultimately, an arrangement will have to be made by which at least some of the oil revenues are diverted to finance the joint economic organisation I have just described; I do not pretend that it will be easy to bring about so great a change from established practice (and some of the rulers who do well out of the present system will certainly object vigorously), but I am convinced that some such change will eventually be forced on both the companies and the governments.

There remains the question of integrating Israel into a joint organisation. For the time being there is probably no hope of that. But there is even less hope of a peaceful settlement while present policies are continued. If political stability can be created among the Arab countries, at least there will be a slackening of tension, and a better atmosphere will be created for tackling the difficult problem of an advanced European-type state in the middle of less developed neighbours who inevitably regard it as an interloper. Given stability, even the Arabs might come to realise in time that the accession of Israel to an economic development organisation would be of advantage, if for no other reason than that she possesses the strongest and most modern economy in the Middle East.

The elements of a long-term policy are thus: first a firm guarantee (working both ways) of something like the present frontiers of Israel; secondly, the assurance that the western powers will work together and not against each other; and thirdly, that they will turn their energies to creating a boldly-conceived organism for economic development on a genuinely international and non-discriminatory basis over which they will seek no political control. Exclusive military and political agreements have no part to play in such a policy. The cautious and the traditionally-minded will say that a policy of this sort offers no guarantee of success. True enough, but the lesson of the last ten years is that present policies offer the certainty of disaster.

V

THE FAR EAST

KENNETH YOUNGER

OLD habits of thought die hard, in international as in other human affairs. History shows many examples of nations continuing in an established relationship to one another long after the basis of the relationship was gone, simply because men's minds were still running along the old grooves. The closing phases of empires have often been prolonged for just this reason, and even when the big change has occurred, the building of a new system has been impeded because old assumptions carry on, sometimes for generations, into the new era.

There is a danger of this happening today in the relations between Asia and the west. For three hundred years and more, a picture has been slowly building up in the minds of Europeans of the the role their countries are destined to play in Asia; and an equally clear picture has formed in the minds of Asians of the treatment they may expect from Europeans and the kind of policies they must follow if they are to become masters of their own fate. Old fashioned thinking is to be found among Asians no less than among Europeans, as well as among some western anti-imperialists, who have done much to bring about the great changes of the last twenty years.

As recently as 1939, in the whole area of Southern Asia, from the Persian Gulf to the China border, there was scarcely an Asian people whose country was not under European rule; and even the rare exceptions, such as Afghanistan or Siam, had retained their independence only because of the rivalry of competing European states, Britain and Russia, or Britain and France. Despite intermittent internal troubles, the European overlords of these territories maintained a pretty firm control, and their anxieties arose far more from the hostility of other European countries than from fear of immediate revolt on the part of the governed. Britain's strategy in particular was based largely upon the determination not only to maintain her own communications with India and the Indian Ocean, but to retain the power to deny access to the area to any European adversary in case of war. So long as the British position in the Middle East held, this was a perfectly practicable policy, and only Russia of all European competitors represented a standing threat owing to her common border with Afghanistan.

The whole of South Asia was thus a colonial or near-colonial area, administered by France, the Netherlands and Portugal as well as Britain, but owing its external security overwhelmingly to British power. Only when one turned the corner, as it were, into the China seas and the Pacific did one find a different picture. Here China retained nominal sovereignty, but for more than half a century suffered various forms of political indignity, economic exploitation and religious offensive at the hands of westerners, before becoming a military victim to the new Asian imperialism of Japan.

Japan, once hopefully eyed by Europeans as yet another profitable trading area, is the one instance of the total failure of western policies in the 19th century. Japan's reaction to the threat of western technology was so powerful that within less than fifty years of her decision to bring herself up to date she had defeated a European power in war, acquired her first colonial territories and established herself as a new and formidable imperialist rival to the western nations. To this day she is far ahead of all her Asian neighbours in industrialisation and technical 'know-how', and it is the example of her victories over western powers from 1941 to 1943 that, more than anything else, has ended the myth of western invincibility in Asia.

It is a further point of significance that only in the Pacific area had the United States played any considerable role or acquired any considerable experience in Asian affairs prior to 1939. In this area she administered a colony—the Philippines. She had been the first to open up Japan to western contacts. She had intervened actively to maintain her influence as against the European powers in China, and had led the missionary effort of the Christian Churches there. Finally her sailors, looking west from Hawaii and Pearl Harbour, were already studying the strategic relevance of east Asia to the defence of the United States.

II

THE transformation accomplished throughout Asia by the second World War and its aftermath has drastically altered the whole balance of world power. The psychological grip which Europe had established upon Asia was too completely broken by the Japanese victories to be capable of restoration when Japan was finally defeated—mainly by the United States. The white imperialists had proved unable to protect their empires, and the inhabitants had seen white troops and civilians taken captive by an Asian power. In many areas there were indigenous authorities anxious to take over power when Japan collapsed. In few areas did a majority want to see the Europeans return at all.

Yet return they did, and the story of the decade of 1945–55 is largely the story of how they had to leave again after all. They did so with varying degrees of foresight and good grace. Britain had by far the biggest stake and took by far the wisest course, in relinquishing her hold on the Indian sub-continent willingly and rapidly. By voluntarily giving up so much so soon, she created entirely new possibilities for an eventual peaceful solution of her own remaining colonial problems and those of her European allies. Whether or not the problems of the Dutch in Indonesia or the French in Indo-China could and should have been handled exactly as the British Labour government handled those of India, it is undeniable that the enforced departure of the Dutch and the French from these territories after so much delay has left political and material troubles behind, which might have been avoided by a more imaginative approach. Whatever the correct apportionment of blame, the political and economic weaknesses of the countries which were formerly French and Dutch colonies come high among the causes of anxiety in south east Asia today.

As a result of these events the Netherlands has virtually ceased to exist as a force in south east Asia, and France is in a fair way to suffer the same fate. Time and Asian pressure will inevitably dispose also of the Portuguese, whose interests in the area her allies need not, perhaps, hasten to destroy, but surely should not 'strive officiously to keep alive'. Of the old colonial powers, therefore, Britain alone retains substantial direct responsibilities, in Malaya, Borneo and Hong Kong. I shall return later to the separate problems which these territories present, contenting myself here with the comment that, while Britain cannot avoid the special responsibilities arising from her position as an administering power, her fundamental interests in the area no longer depend mainly on this fact, but rather upon her common interest, along with many other countries, in promoting peace and freedom to trade in the area.

This is not to say, of course, that there are not great British economic interests at stake, and indeed many Asians remain convinced that Britain's only interest in Malaya is the retention of her property in tin and rubber. In general, however, Britain's economic interest in the area should not be seen primarily as one of British property rights (for on a fair balance Malaya owes Britain nothing), still less as the right of a colonial power to direct the use of resources. The interest of Britain, as of other trading nations, is that the possibilities of free intercourse between south east Asia and the west should remain after the ending of colonial régimes. The proposition which seemed to give Stalin so much satisfaction in his last major article in 1952—that the success of communism would accentuate the division of the world into mutually exclusive market areas—is not one which the west can willingly accept, and it is in south east Asia that this issue might arise in its sharpest form.

Outside the former colonial areas, post-war changes have been, if possible, more dramatic still. Western influence in China has come to an end and there is a real possibility that the coming decades may see the assertion by China of her own ideological and material leadership throughout the whole of east Asia. How far she will succeed in this must obviously depend upon the progress she makes with her own internal reconstruction and industrial development. Her plans are ambitious and her confidence high. She starts, it is true, from a low level of material well-being and technical skill. But it seems likely that her government will be capable of imposing strong discipline upon her people, and the deep and solid foundations of Chinese culture may well make her people highly adaptable to the new techniques which they will be called upon to master. No western plans should be based upon an assumption that the Chinese bid for leadership is likely to fail.

It no longer seems possible that Japan could re-establish her leadership in the form which she had promised herself in the pre-war East Asian Co-prosperity Sphere. In that sense Japan seems to have missed the tide of history—if indeed the tide was ever really running so high for her. The possibility, however, of a new 'co-prosperity sphere', based on a partnership between China and Japan is certainly not excluded from all Japanese minds. What the Chinese think about it we do not yet know, but their decision will be of the first importance. Should they wish to do so, they could probably open up for Japan a long-term prospect of a share in Asian trade and influence far more seductive to that country than her present dependence upon the United States. If, however, they insist that cooperation of this kind must await the communisation of Japan, the day of fulfilment will certainly be postponed, and dangerous upheavals in the Far East seem likely to occur before any stable new order is achieved.

When thinking of the possibility of Chinese leadership in Asia, it is as well for westerners to remember that they themselves are not serious competitors in this field. The problem is to fill the vacuum left by the decline of European imperialism, and no new form of European or American leadership will be accepted by Asians in replacement. It is perhaps in this sphere that out-of-date thinking among both westerners and Asians is most evident. Even westerners who are innocent of any hangover of colonial superiority, above all the Americans, tend to assume too readily that western standards, just because much of Asia has been absorbing them for centuries, must still have an irresistible appeal to Asian minds. The truth is, however, that, technology apart, Asians are at present in a state of positive revolt against western standards and are even making their own contribution to out-of-date thinking by insisting that western colonialism is still the greatest danger to peace in Asia. This is, to put it mildly, an exaggeration, but it is a deeply ingrained idea and it unites innumerable Asians among whom agreement on other topics is hard to find. Whether well or ill founded, it is a contemporary fact which is of importance in framing western policies for the area.

In these circumstances the limitation placed upon Chinese

leadership of Asia seems far more likely to depend upon the emergence of India as a rival pole of attraction than upon the success of the west in promoting the adoption in Asia of its own combination of parliamentary democracy and free enterprise, either by means of a liberal expenditure of dollars or by the pursuit of nuclear strategy.

III

THE basic problems which fall to be solved in the Far East are, at least, in their origin, quite independent of the cold war. The end of colonial rule in so many areas was certain to occur in some not very distant future. That it has happened in mid-century instead of some twenty to fifty years later is the result of the reverses suffered by the colonial powers in the second World War and owes nothing either to the rise of strong communist states or to communist agitation within the colonial territories.

In India, British rule had for many years looked forward to the time when Britain would withdraw, and although there were, of course, powerful elements in British political life which had thought of this as a distant event, the political policies followed by the government of India had made it inevitable that the goal would be reached sooner rather than later. This being so, it was inconceivable that other dependent countries in Asia could be held indefinitely by their European rulers.

No socialist will shed tears over this trend of events, which is fully in accord with what the socialist movement in all countries has preached and worked for over many years. It is true that the liquidation of existing colonial régimes has not always turned out to be quite as simple an operation as some socialists had supposed. An example is Malaya—where British rule had radically altered the whole nature of Malayan society but without providing a framework of government which could readily have taken over the control of the multi-racial population if British authority had been abruptly withdrawn after 1945. Even here, however, only a moderate time-lag and not a departure from principle has been involved.

Similarly the awakening of the desire of Asian peoples for a better material existence, their determination to develop their natural resources and to share in the technical advantages of the

west are all phenomena which socialists must welcome, no matter what uncomfortable social consequences they may have, or
how in the longer run they may shift the balance of world
power against the west. Western socialists would wish to be
considered partners of the Asian peoples in their endeavours,
and see it as one of their main tasks to influence the policies of
their own governments in this direction.

The emergence of China as a great power poses, in the context of the present world situation, a somewhat more complicated problem. That China should, after so long a decline, show
signs of demanding a leading position in the affairs of the Far
East and of the world is, in itself, no more than the assertion of a
claim which her ancient culture, her vast and industrious population and her as yet scarcely tapped resources fully entitle her
to make. It is thus no more reasonable to resent China's new
importance than India's; nor are the xenophobic aspects of present Chinese policy more than an intensification of what every
'old China hand' expected from the first strong and confident
Chinese government that might appear after the defeat of
Japan.

On the other hand, great power held in the hands of men
whose motives are imperfectly known is bound to cause anxiety
to all whom that power may affect, and in the interdependent
world of today that means virtually everyone. Revolutionary
governments, when they first achieve power, are always apt to
be awkward neighbours, self-assertive, quick to detect real or
imagined insults, and accustomed by their training to use and
expect violence as a means of settling their quarrels.

How far these dangerous characteristics can be softened by
wise handling on the part of other powers is hard to say, for
there are few historical precedents to guide us, and the attitude
of the west to the Chinese communist revolution is a question
which, more than any other, has divided British from American
policy. The story of this dispute since the Chinese communists
got control of China at the end of 1949 is too well known to
stand detailed repetition. Some analysis of the causes of the divergence is, however, relevant for the light it throws on the
alternative policies which might be followed today.

IV

APOLOGISTS for United States policy towards China usually reply to criticism by saying that the Chinese took part in the Korean War, that there is a resolution of the United Nations still in force which condemns them as aggressors, and that their conduct in a score of incidents, such as the conviction of United States fliers for espionage, unfits them to be treated as normal members of international society. Emotionally all this adds up to something quite effective, and the American case is essentially emotional.

There is truth in many of the accusations which Americans level against the government of Peking, but this does not explain why United States policy differs from that of Britain, of most Asian countries, and of a number of other states, including some who fought in the Korean War. That the American attitude is not basically the result of the Korean War or of any misdemeanours which may have been committed in the last five years by the Chinese communists is shown by the fact that the United States had taken up its position before the Korean War broke out, that it was careful at the time of the truce negotiations to state that the end of the fighting would not alter its attitude to China, and that there are powerful forces in American politics which have been deeply committed to maintaining this position regardless of Chinese behaviour. It is characteristic that those Americans who cry out most loudly that 'the communists must not be allowed to shoot their way into the United Nations' come predominantly from precisely those circles which have always cared least for the United Nations and would not be found leaping to its defence in any other context.

The United States has so far always been able to secure substantial majorities in the United Nations for its China policy, but everyone knows that of all the governments which think it politic to support the American position, very few except Syngman Rhee and Chiang Kai Shek believe it to be wise. It is not hard to see why these two personalities support it, because each has been deeply concerned to lead the United States into a major war in China. This, however, is not at all in the interests of the United States, whose motives in the matter are far more complex and go some way back into history.

In the first place there has always been much idealism in the American attitude to China, from the great efforts of American missionaries, and the supposedly disinterested policy of the 'Open Door in China', to the UNRRA aid given to China after the war and the idealisation of both Chiang Kai Shek and his clever and beautiful wife. Nothing is so bitter as affection turned sour, and the disillusionment when the new masters of China rejected American friendship was bitter indeed.

Secondly the whole issue became the plaything of American party politics, until it was a matter of faith among Republicans that Chiang had been betrayed by Truman, Acheson and Marshall and must now be supported by all honest men. Plenty of people had an interest in keeping this myth alive. These sentiments fitted in well with the anti-communist crusade which was sweeping America and with the theme of liberating the peoples already under communist control, including even the Soviet people. Americans went to far greater extremes in this than others, partly no doubt because of their greater consciousness of power, but largely because the idea that there may be bad situations with which one has to live patiently for long periods, unable to set things right yet not regarding them as disastrous, is as unfamiliar to Americans as it is familiar to other people who have lived cheek by jowl with difficult neighbours for centuries.

Lastly it is important to emphasise that to many Americans China and Japan are not so much the easternmost parts of Asia as the western limit of the Pacific Ocean. Since the experience of the recent war, American strategists have developed the theory that an 'island chain' stretching from the Aleutians through Japan to Formosa and the Philippines is an essential part of United States security. This conception, coupled with the conviction, widely held in some service circles, that an all-out war with communism in the near future was inevitable, naturally led Americans after 1950 to think of the Far East mainly in military terms, and to take a relatively short view of all problems. For what was the use of political subtleties or regard for Asian susceptibilities, if the whole area was to be plunged into major war within two or three years?

Not one of these American attitudes had its parallel in Britain.

On most, British thinking was the exact opposite. The British, far from seeing the old China through rose-coloured glasses, had no illusions either about Chiang Kai Shek or about the likely attitude of any new Chinese government to foreigners in general and westerners in particular. If the Chinese revolution took a form that was unwelcome to us, that was no great surprise and we quickly accepted it as a fact. The Labour Government gave a firm lead on this in 1950, and there has subsequently been no party political dispute about it in Britain and no divergence between left-wing politicians and Far Eastern traders and business men.

There was, equally, no toying with the idea of reversing the communist victories in the huge territories of China and Russia. This was no doubt partly due to the knowledge that Britain had no resources with which any such grandiose crusade could be attempted; but even apart from that, the whole doctrine of an early inevitable war with the communist bloc was rejected by all classes in Britain. Britain therefore viewed with scepticism the American talk of the 'island chain'. Among British service chiefs there has always been doubt whether the security of the United States really depends upon a string of bases so far from America,* and whether in any case a policy which takes so little account of the close ties which Japan must have with Asia is likely to succeed in holding indefinitely the most important islands in the chain—the Japanese islands themselves.

More significant than all this is that British people reach the Far East not by crossing the Pacific, but by way of India and Singapore. British thinking on all Asia was largely formed in India. British experience of nationalism there, despite the non-communist form Indian nationalism has taken, has deeply coloured British views on the Chinese revolution. It is seen as the culmination of a long historical process which no western power is going to stop and which no substantial body of Asians will cooperate in stopping.

Aggression outside Chinese borders is another matter, and on this British policy is not open to the charges of 'appeasement' so often levelled by Americans. British policy is, however, less

*Americans have felt similar scepticism about British bases in the Middle East.

concerned to build up military positions against an early war than to build a political relationship of trust between Asia and the west. No one in Britain believes that Chinese expansionism, if this is what China intends, can be checked for long except with Asian support. It follows that policies directed against China and based on thinking which Asians do not share are felt to be unreal and in the long run doomed to failure. In particular, policies which demand of Asians that they should adopt postures of undisguised hostility to the new China are asking the impossible of Japan as much as of India and south east Asia. Only Chiang Kai Shek, Syngman Rhee and possibly the Philippine government might accept this American proposition, and all three are well outside the main stream of Asian development, commanding little authority but what the United States may choose to lend them.

For several years now the developing situation, both in the Far East and in American domestic politics, has been slowly bringing United States policy nearer to those of her allies. The *débacle* of American diplomacy at the 1954 Geneva Conference on Indo-China no doubt contributed to the painful process. As already stated, there are now plenty of leading personalities in both American parties who understand what ought to be done. Their difficulty is that rash statements made in the past and rash undertakings, especially those made to Chiang Kai Shek, have committed American prestige to positions which are hard to hold but now almost equally hard to relinquish without humiliation. All through the early part of 1955 the world watched the spectacle of the Administration trying to rationalise its position in the Formosa straits, but frustrated at every turn by the need to combine in one and the same statement assurances to the world that the offshore islands were not considered indispensable and that Chiang Kai Shek was no longer considered as a potential ruler of China, with contrary assurances both to Chiang Kai Shek himself and to Senator Knowland.

It is hardly surprising that even the subtlest draftsmanship did not prove quite equal to this task, and that the world was kept on tenterhooks lest an unnecessary clash of arms between the United States and China should be allowed to occur. It is an ironical fact that most of America's allies relied at that time more upon the restraining influence of the Soviet Union upon her Chinese ally than upon American wisdom to prevent this dispute from setting the spark to a major Far Eastern war. In the latter half of 1955 this controversy faded from the newspaper headlines, but it is hard to believe that it will not be revived at some time. It is therefore disquieting that United States policy has so far seemed to be stricken with immobility, and that the opportunity to disengage from weak and dangerous positions has not been taken.

V

IT is not difficult to state in general terms the way in which British socialists seek to adjust the relationship between Britain and the Far East. They recognise the end of Britain's claim to privileged positions and superior status over the peoples of the area. They recognise that the change must be rapid and complete, but they wish to see a smooth transition which will not destroy what is mutually beneficial in the relations between Britain and Asia, a conception which will include the continuance of trade and of cultural and scientific interchange. Above all they will wish, in the period of drastic change, to maintain the principles laid down in the United Nations Charter that international disputes must be solved by peaceful means and that armed aggression must be resisted.

Britain's experience in south Asia has led her to believe that a policy of this kind can be successful. The governments of such countries as India, Burma and Indonesia, though yielding to none in their determination to throw off all forms of western domination, have shown that they also see advantages in this conception.

For such a policy to succeed, cooperation from both sides is indispensable, and it is by no means to be assumed that communist governments in Asia accept any of the assumptions made by western socialists, except that the period of western domination is coming to an end. The intellectual training of communists, so far from leading them to believe in peaceful change, makes them profoundly sceptical of its possibility. And when, as in India, an apparently major shift of power occurs in a peaceful manner, their instinct is to believe that the change must be unreal or at least superficial. They are not content with the transfer of power from Europeans to Asians unless at the same time the new Asian state takes on a communist form. On these terms normal and friendly relations between newly independent Asian states and the western world are likely to be established only with great difficulty.

The attitude of the People's Government in China since 1949 supports this view. Not even India has been able to establish a relation with the new China which could be called normal, while the Chinese have treated all western powers as hostile regardless of their actual conduct. The British Government's attempt to deal reasonably with China, even at the risk of friction with its American ally, has not been paralleled by any greater readiness on the Chinese side to reach agreement with Britain than with the United States, or by any less drastic treatment of British citizens and interests in China.

Added to this, the original refusal of the majority in the United Nations to recognise the change of government in China, and the subsequent clash between the United Nations and Chinese forces in Korea, have led Communist China to regard the United Nations as an American-controlled body, hostile to herself, and have increased her disposition to rely on her own strength alone in order to obtain her ends. Whether her attitude would have been different if she had been accepted in the United Nations from the start is something which will always be argued but cannot now be proved.

For one school of thought the simple deduction from this is that any accommodation with a major communist power such as China is impossible, and that the only sensible course for the west is to prepare for the war that is bound to come. Some have even advocated the disabling of the communist powers before they can attain parity in weapons of mass destruction. Advocates of this type of policy have been found in quite high places in the United States though fortunately they have never yet been able to dominate official policy. In Britain there has been no significant support for anything of the kind, and accordingly no time will be spent in discussing it here, especially since the moment for such a policy has in any case passed.

What we have rather to consider is how far we can hope, by

reasonable trade policies and patient diplomacy, to establish a tolerable relationship with the new China; and what our attitude should be to the expansion of Chinese influence beyond the borders of China proper, above all in south east Asia and Japan.

On the first of these questions there is little to say except that we must do our best to establish a tolerable relationship with China and see what results we get. Having decided against participation in any crusade to undo the Chinese revolution, we have no clear choice of alternative courses before us. We must seek normal relations by every possible means and hope for some response. If we get none that will not be our fault and we shall have lost nothing by trying. An immediate requirement of this policy is a modification of the discriminatory restrictions on trade with China.

On the second question there is no use in concealing from ourselves that, in the present mood of China, the spread of Chinese influence, in any form approximating to control, is likely to have consequences disadvantageous to ourselves. It is likely to involve the dropping of an iron curtain or at least a severe restriction of trading and other relationships between ourselves and the area newly controlled by China. It does not follow that trade will cease, any more than trade with China itself has ceased, but the economy of the area will probably be closely integrated with that of China and its other external trade will become confined, as has been the case in Eastern Europe, to the limited range of commodities for which the communist bloc of countries provides no outlet or can offer no adequate supply. The availability, for instance, of south east Asian rice, rubber or tin for the world at large would be highly uncertain.

China's intentions in relation to eastern Asia as a whole are, as has already been said, largely unknown. There is however, little doubt that she wishes as a minimum to see an end to western colonialism and to United States military bases anywhere in the area. Her philosophy being what it is, she may be expected to promote these objectives in the only way which seems to her sure—that is by the total elimination of western influence, in all and not merely in colonial or military forms, and the substitution of her own. In other words it is abdication by the west of all traditional or contemporary associations, rather than a reasonable accommodation, for which she is likely to work. There is, however, no indication that she is determined to achieve her ends by naked military aggression, while equally there can be no guarantee to the contrary.

On the face of it there seems every reason why she should be prepared to show patience in any expansionist plans she may have. In the first place the pre-condition for any lasting Chinese sphere of influence is clearly the building of a strong modern economy in China itself, and this is still in its earliest and most precarious stage. In the second place, she has other non-military methods available to her which might well relieve her of the necessity of facing a direct trial of strength with other great powers. Her prestige in East Asia is already high. There are in many countries strong Chinese minorities, whose loyalty to the Chinese homeland will probably grow automatically as Chinese strength grows, no matter what the political complexion of the régime. There are also sympathetic communist minorities in many areas, coupled with unstable régimes based upon out-of-date political and economic systems. Though there is no evidence that any country, with the possible exception of Viet-Nam, would at present be ready to embrace communism by a democratically-taken decision, there is equally no deep hostility to China or even to communist ideas, so that the ground is favourable for political infiltration and eventual subversion of existing régimes.

In Japan the situation is, from the Chinese point of view, far less advanced. Though the Japanese may be impressed by events in China, their strong national sentiment, their technical superiority over the Chinese and all other Asians and their closely-knit social structure makes them a far tougher proposition, as they are a far more valuable prize. A military assault seems about the last way in which the communist powers would choose to tackle the Japanese problem. It is rather upon Japan's need for trade relations with Asia and her reluctance to remain a mere satellite in the American constellation that the Chinese and the Soviet Union are likely to concentrate their efforts to win her to their side.

Throughout the whole area of the Far East it seems that we must consider the new China as a power which wishes no good to the west in Asia, but is likely, though not certain, to refrain from direct military aggression against her neighbours. Western socialists may therefore consider the Far Eastern problem as one not so much of military security as of competition between Chinese communism on the one hand and a more democratic form of socialism on the other for the allegiance of the uncommitted peoples of Asia. In facing this competition it is pointless to sentimentalise over the new China, which will certainly be a formidable and probably a hostile rival. There is however no need either for the catastrophism of those who think that the contest must inevitably end in war, or for the defeatism which assumes that all Asia is bound to choose the communist path. For western socialists the Asian situation presents above all a challenge to themselves to prod their countries into a policy of active cooperation with the peoples of Asia, and into a realisation of the urgency of liquidating the colonial question and of the scale of effort required to meet the social and economic necessities of Asia today. To meet this challenge western policy must be many-sided, imaginative and fast-moving.

VI

THE principles which should inspire British colonial policy are reasonably clear, but the application of these principles varies widely from one territory to another.

Sarawak, North Borneo and Brunei are all territories whose future seems of necessity to lie in some form of association with other territories rather than in complete national independence. This association seems likely to be with Britain for some time to come, if only because there is no demand for association with anyone else, and no one else who seems capable of giving them the assistance they need in their present stage of development. This situation however should not be allowed to breed complacency. It is unlikely that even the most quiescent territories will indefinitely escape from the impact of events around them, and no area is more likely to see drastic change in the next decade than the one in which these small colonies are situated. They are at present politically backward and have an inadequate economic base. There is some danger that, if their patriarchal calm should be rudely disturbed, we should see the all too familiar spectacle of a colonial power protesting its theoretical willingness to move with the times, but in practice compelled to maintain its paternalistic authority because of the absence of any politically trained native personnel or informed public opinion capable of maintaining even the essentials of civilised government. Should such a situation develop, the highly emotive anti-colonial cry could be used with great effect to discredit Britain throughout the whole area. It is therefore essential for Britain to set the pace herself and not merely to be dragged along by events.

Hong Kong presents in every respect a unique problem. She is a tiny territory, tightly packed with a purely Chinese population, yet run by a benevolent, progressive and wholly undemocratic British administration. Her *raison d'être* is commercial, and she is dependent for the livelihood of her people on intercourse not only with the Chinese mainland, of which she is virtually a part, but with the traders of the world at large. Regardless of what her political status might be, she would have to remain in fact an international port or else unload a large part of her population on to other areas.

These hard facts about Hong Kong are no doubt the main reason why the Chinese communists, despite their strongly nationalistic attitude to such territories as Formosa, have as yet exerted little pressure against Hong Kong. The present position in Hong Kong probably suits them well, and any change would deprive them of a useful window on the world and be economically burdensome to them—unless they themselves were to try to maintain Hong Kong as an international trading centre on something like existing lines, a very difficult and uncertain proposition for them to undertake.

It may well be that the Chinese will decide to let time solve the question of Hong Kong for them. Despite the long-standing nationalist demand for Hong Kong, which the Americans and some Commonwealth governments were ready to support in 1945, the Chinese have a slender moral claim upon Hong Kong itself, which was a barren unpopulated rock when ceded to Britain in 1842, and owes all its development to British enterprise. In any case the lease of the new territories, which have a growing population together with essential installations and some 60 per cent of the colony's water supplies, expires in 1997. In order to acquire title to this part of Hong Kong the Chinese have only to wait and announce that they prefer not to renew the lease. Moreover, they have only to let their intention be known well in advance in order to ensure that the coming transfer of sovereignty casts its shadow a long way ahead. It is difficult to suppose that large numbers of the Chinese in Hong Kong are not even now preparing to come to terms with their mainland neighbours if the need should arise. In any case, the Communist Party operates legally in Hong Kong, so that psychological preparation of some sections at least of the Hong Kong population may be assumed to be taking place all the time.

In such circumstances it is hard to believe that the question so often posed 'Would Britain fight for Hong Kong?' has much reality. If the Chinese decided that they wanted to end western rule, there as elsewhere, they would possess powerful means for securing this objective without firing a shot. On the British side a purely military defence of Hong Kong would be justifiable only if the population clearly wished to be militarily defended and was willing, in its vast majority, to take its part in the defence. Though some, no doubt, would wish to fight against the prospect of communist rule, they would have little that was positive to fight for, since a Hong Kong reduced permanently to a besieged fortress would be no place for a civilian population running into millions.

So far as the practicability of defending Hong Kong is concerned, although there are perhaps conditions in which this would be conceivable, it would surely involve something more than the purely static defence of the perimeter of the colony itself. In other words it could only be envisaged as part of a more extended war. It is not clear who would be willing to line up with the British in an extended war for the defence of Hong Kong. Certainly the Americans and Canadians would be very reluctant starters. The people of Britain and of Hong Kong itself would, I think, be equally unenthusiastic.

It is usually considered bad form or at best irresponsible to give expression to these thoughts, but they are in everyone's mind and their weight is not seriously disputed, even by those who refuse to draw what seems to be the obvious deduction from them—that the future of Hong Kong will depend upon the general relationship between Britain and China, and that British attention should be fixed upon this rather than upon romantic notions of a last-ditch defence of Britain's Far Eastern heritage.

The problems in Malaya are far better known, and centre round the multi-racial nature of the population. The so-called 'emergency' has been kept up almost entirely by a small minority of one race only, the Chinese, and has never seemed to approximate to a national movement.

Large-scale security measures involving a considerable military effort have restricted the areas of violence, and may continue to do so. There is, however, little reason to think that the rebels will be wholly eliminated unless either the communist leadership receives orders from Peking to give up the fight, or the local population of Malaya, including the Malayan Chinese, themselves decide to take the lead and turn the defeat of the rebels into a patriotic duty—which is only likely to occur when they themselves have to shoulder responsibility for law and order in the country. This is already happening in the Federation, and it would be folly to allow Singapore to lag far behind.

The political pace has been constantly accelerating in Malaya. Where even in 1955 the talk was of independence within a period which might be as long as ten years, internal self-government is now an immediate issue, and the right to claim full independence cannot be delayed for long.

How soon the right will be exercised and what decisions will be freely taken with regard to Commonwealth membership, the future of the Singapore base and other aspects of security, can at present only be a matter of speculation. Much will presumably depend upon the attitude of the Malayan Communist Party, with whom the leaders of the Federation and of Singapore failed to reach a settlement at the first truce talks in January 1956.

It would be wrong to minimise the inherent dangers of the Malayan situation, where several millions of overseas Chinese, entrenched in the business world and in the schools and unions of Singapore, have not yet fully revealed their intentions for the future. Whatever the uncertainties, however, the course for Britain is fairly clear, in the sense that she must now prefer the

risk of entrusting to elected authorities the greatest possible
measure of responsibility to the graver risk of discouraging the
genuinely democratic movement which is now moving into
positions of power.

VII

WHILE colonial policy is peculiarly a British responsibility, the
economic approach to south east Asia involves, by contrast, the
cooperation of many countries, both inside and outside the area.
To some westerners the economic problem seems important
mainly, if not solely, on account of its relevance to the defeat of
communism, but to the countries concerned the raising of living
standards and the development of modern techniques are ends
in themselves, desirable on grounds of human dignity and welfare. In so far as external considerations affect the drive of Asians
for economic betterment, their determination is to end their
dependence on more advanced powers rather than to take sides
in the Cold War.

There has always been a danger that these conflicting motives
would make it difficult to persuade the richer countries, especially the United States, to contribute adequate economic aid in a
form in which Asian countries would be willing to accept it;
and western assistance has been refused more than once when it
carried an implication of support for western anti-communist
policies. This difficulty, however, has been largely surmounted
by the cooperative techniques developed through the Colombo
Plan. This plan, initiated by Australia with strong British backing in 1950, and now extended to include the United States in
addition to all the countries of south east Asia, has proved acceptable to countries receiving aid, who do not see in it any
reflection upon their independence; and it gives reasonable assurance to countries providing aid that their contributions will
be spent upon worth-while and practicable projects. Despite its
dissociation from cold war strategy, the plan has commended
itself to many leading Americans in both political parties, so that
it now seems possible that a programme of increased United
States aid for south east Asia may be carried out through the
machinery of the plan.

That such a programme is needed and that the scale of international assistance is becoming increasingly inadequate can scarcely be questioned. Living standards are desperately low, and ever wider circles in Asian countries are resolved to raise them. Yet the possibility of the Asian countries themselves raising by democratic methods all the finance required from their own domestic savings is almost nil. A United Nations committee of experts calculated in 1951 that domestic savings would fall short by more than $5,000 million of what is needed each year to raise *per caput* income by only 2 per cent per annum. This is more than ten times the total annual aid originally planned under the Colombo Plan, and although external aid from all sources has increased to some extent, the gap to be filled remains very great. Unless western policies are directed to reducing the gap, there will either be no social progress in south east Asia, or else the active elements in south east Asian society will decide to put their faith in the draconian methods of financing development of which communist China is providing an example at once impressive and forbidding.

It may indeed be argued that Asia's political future will turn less upon military considerations than upon the ability of India to show by her example that the methods of the 'open society' which she practises can produce the development which all Asia is seeking, and that they can produce it on a scale rivalling communist China, and at far less human cost. This issue, which has been described by Mr. Chester Bowles as 'the battle of our century',* will clearly be decided above all by India herself. Nevertheless there is much that the west can do, both by technical aid and the provision of capital, to help India in surmounting the initial difficulties of capital formation which face every country embarking upon industrial development.

Pleas for a great increase in aid to south east Asia have usually been met by the statement that it is not lack of funds but lack of technical skills and adequate administrative resources which have been holding up progress. This has no doubt been true in the past, but the basis has now been laid, through the cooperation of the Colombo Plan and the United Nations agencies, for an increasing application of capital from abroad. It is therefore time

*Chester Bowles: *The New Dimensions of Peace.* (Harper Bros. New York 1955, p. 165).

that the provision of this capital became a major preoccupation
of the western powers.

An equally important and perhaps even more difficult line of
approach to Asia's economic difficulties would be an attempt to
introduce some stability into the world prices of the few primary products upon which the countries so largely depend, notably rice, rubber, tin, copra and petroleum products. The fluc-
tuations in rubber and tin prices in recent years have been
particularly violent, and most of the changes have been directly
attributable to the policies of the United States, which is by far
the largest outside consumer of the products of the area.

This is not the place to enter into an argument on the general
question of international stabilisation of commodity prices.
What must be said, however, is that the benefit to the area of an
assured market for its exports for some years ahead at reasonably steady prices would probably do more to promote peace
and economic progress than even very large increases in the
quantities of external aid. Since the main commodities involved
are few in number, and the country which determines their
prices is, overwhelmingly, the United States, some improvement upon the present position could probably be achieved if
the United States could follow a policy of long-term bulk agreements with the area. Britain should, in any case, play as big a
part in such a policy as the scale of British demand permits,
while recognising that the effects would be somewhat limited
unless the United States were to do the same. It is, perhaps, in
this field more than in any other that competition will have to
be met from the Soviet Union and China, who will be in a
position to make attractive offers of trade to an economically
self-governing Malaya.

VIII

ECONOMIC policies unfold themselves over a period of years.
They would have no opportunity to develop if interrupted by
external military aggression.

Something has already been said of the possible attitude of
China in this matter, and the deduction has been drawn that
direct military aggression against south east Asia is unlikely to
form any part of her plans. If this is correct, it follows that polit-

ical and economic policy should take priority over military policy. It does not follow, however, that military considerations can be wholly disregarded, for there are many different circumstances which might lead to the use of armed force against some part of south east Asia, and the existence of reasonable defensive arrangements may be both an essential deterrent to aggression and—as we have found in Europe—an essential pre-condition for creating political confidence in the area.

That there are, however, very narrow limits to what can at present usefully be done in the military sphere emerges clearly from the early experience of the South East Asia Treaty Organisation (SEATO). This was a body conceived in the United States, following the military reverses in Indo-China, and brought to an uneasy birth with wholly inadequate Asian support and the reluctant acquiescence of Britain. India, Indonesia and Burma stood out of it altogether. Pakistan and the Philippines joined in, more in pursuance of their overall cooperation with the United States than for any addition the treaty gave to their own security. Australia was keen on it because it seemed likely to increase American military involvement in the south west Pacific, and also values it today as an agency for joint planning with some at any rate of the Asian governments. Of Asian countries, however, only Siam, undoubtedly one of the most vulnerable spots in south east Asia, showed real enthusiasm.

It was thus apparent from the first that SEATO did not in fact bring new Asian resources to the defence of south east Asia. Moreover it did something to split the so-called 'Colombo Powers' politically without bringing any fresh contribution from the only outside powers with the means to help—U.S.A., Britain, Australia and New Zealand. The traditional United States reluctance to commit any American troops to the mainland of Asia in peacetime is paralleled by a reluctance on the Asian side to see western troops back in their countries, so that effective joint military planning in the area, beyond what Commonwealth countries could in any case have done under the ANZAM agreement, is difficult. The upshot has so far been little more than a few staff conferences and an American announcement that any Chinese aggression in the area will be met by action not only on the spot but in north and central China, and that the forces used will be drawn from the mobile units which the United States maintains at various points in the Far East and south west Pacific. This, it will be seen, has little or nothing to do with a collective defence effort in south east Asia itself, and is merely a particular application of the world-wide United States conception of massive retaliation 'by means and at places of our own choosing'.

So far as Britain is concerned, she is bound, of course, to shoulder responsibility for the defence of the territories she administers; but to undertake further paper commitments in the area could only be misleading, since Britain's power to send substantial further forces to this area is negligible—and the higher the general tension throughout the world, the less would be her power to do so.

These reflections on the military prospects in south east Asia will seem unduly depressing only to those who persist in thinking of that part of the world as predominantly a military problem. Effective local defence anywhere in the world depends on people's willingness to defend themselves, and this willingness is absent from most of south east Asia, while distance from the main centres of western power makes western intervention costly and difficult. If full scale aggression occurred, therefore, the military outlook would indeed be bleak: but since that would almost certainly imply general war in the Far East it is simply a part of the general problem of world security in the nuclear age.

The true defence against communist expansion by means short of direct military aggression lies in the political and economic field, where Britain still has a leading role to play and at least some of the means with which to play it. The danger, which cannot be too often stressed, lies in a tendency to think of south east Asian problems in terms different from those in which they are seen by south east Asians themselves. This is a sure recipe for disaster, since there are no forces that can now be mobilised in Asia for a purely western point of view. SEATO comes near to illustrating this thesis. As a declaration that aggression would be resisted it may have had a fleeting value, but it is not a promising line of advance and no great hopes should be reposed in it. It seems very unlikely, for instance, that the future of Viet-Nam, perhaps the most sensitive area in south east Asia just now, will depend in any way upon the progress of this particular organisation.

IX

PERHAPS the most difficult subject for prophecy in all the Far East today is Japan. What is certain is that she has a population rising towards 100 millions, that she is the most industrially advanced country in Asia, and that her people have shown powers of collective effort which ensure that she will again find a place for herself in Far Eastern affairs.

At the present time she does not see clearly how this is to be done, and she is feeling her way with caution. She will not let go of her post-war American connections until she sees other ways open to her of earning a living. What she will probably attempt is to retain her American connections while building new ones with the continent of Asia.

The key to her policy today is her need for world trade. The proportion of her foreign trade which goes to south east Asia is larger than before the war, while her Chinese trade is less. Access to south east Asia is vital to her, and if that area were to go behind an iron or bamboo curtain, it would probably not be long before Japan followed. She also wants trade with China, though how great this possibility will be in the near future is a matter of dispute.

It is clear from this that Japan is more interested than almost any other country in a lowering of tension and a breaking down of barriers in the Far East. Though her present rulers do not want to see south east Asia become communist, they would certainly not join a military organisation for its defence against China, though they might well participate in a system of guarantees in which India and China both participated.

It would clearly be folly for Britain to try to dissuade Japan from widening her relations with the Asian mainland. A purely western orientation is in the long run impossible for her; her trading needs make her a world power requiring access to markets and materials everywhere, preferably on both sides of the iron curtain, and we should welcome her success in doing this.

Britain is inevitably one of Japan's leading trade rivals, and old memories of unfair trading have made it hard for Britain to welcome Japan back into the world community. It is reasonable enough that Britain should retain as many good cards in her hand as possible in her dealings with Japan, and her caginess about Japan's entry into the General Agreement on Tariffs and Trade (GATT) can be justified on that ground. British Labour, however, if it is to sustain a constructive Far Eastern policy, will have to steel itself against the pressure of sectional interests in Britain such as those which have tended to unite Lancashire members of Parliament regardless of party in a fierce protectionism whenever Japanese cotton is mentioned. It would, in any case, be dangerous to make any other assumption than that Japan will continue to expand her exports in many markets, that some of these will be in British colonial markets, and that some of the expansion will be at the expense of British traders. Provided the general level of world trade is rising, this need not involve serious dislocations. In a slump the position, like so many others, would become very dangerous. The fact remains, however, that many millions of poverty stricken people in Asia and Africa want cheap goods, and if Japan can supply them we cannot stand in the way. Provided this is accepted, a certain tactical toughness in holding Japan to accepted trade practices is entirely in order.

It is in the trading field that British and Japanese policy come most directly into contact. In more general matters Britain's means of intervention in the Far East are too limited to permit much freedom of action for our diplomacy. Nevertheless we have, perhaps, more assets than meet the eye. Our long Far Eastern tradition and our post-war Asian policy give us a standing which Japan is inclined to respect, while the fact that we are not held primarily accountable for the post-war occupation gives us certain advantages over the United States in the present phase of Japanese sentiment. British Far Eastern policy since 1949, unlike the American, has always consciously attempted to leave a place in which Japan could live and breathe, for we have seen this as an indispensable condition of Far Eastern peace. Despite our lack of material leverage, therefore, we can hope that our counsels will be listened to with respect, and even a certain friendliness, in this critical period while Japan is slowly moving towards important decisions on her future orientation in the world.

X

IT is not only in relation to Japan that British statesmanship has to consider carefully the means at her disposal for achieving her objectives. The forces which are on the move in the Far East are gigantic. There are huge populations, huge but as yet undeveloped material resources, and explosive ideas in the air. Within the area itself there are major powers, India, China and Japan. The Soviet Union, herself partly a Far East Asian country, and Australia are only just off-stage and are directly concerned with developments in various parts of the area; while the United States, though far away, has become deeply involved as a result of the second World War, and disposes of considerable military and economic resources with which to make her presence felt. The effective weight of all these countries in Far Eastern affairs is likely to grow as the years go by, with the sole exception of the United States, which seems more likely to follow a long-term policy of moderate disengagement, while still retaining a close interest in some aspects of the area.

It is important to see Britain's Far Eastern role in this perspective. Britain is even further away than the United States and has far slighter resources to spare for intervention. By herself she cannot hope to exert a decisive influence. Yet she has a deep interest in the peaceful development of the area because of her concern for Australian and New Zealand security, because of her remaining colonial responsibilities, for economic reasons, and above all, because wrong policies in the Far East could set the spark for a third world war.

It must therefore be the aim of Britain to harness the strength of others as well as her own in support of the concepts which she believes to be sound. In the present phase the problem presents itself above all as one of securing the cooperation both of India and of the United States. In the long run policies in non-communist Asia have little chance of success unless they are at least tacitly accepted by India, while in the short run policies of adequate scale cannot be effective unless backed by American resources.

This being so, one has only to consider the divergent attitudes of India and the United States over Far Eastern matters to realise the difficulties which face British diplomacy. Yet Britain is

uniquely placed to help in harmonising the discordant voices of
her two friends, by virtue of her policy towards China, of her
Commonwealth ties with India and of the peculiar intimacy of
the Anglo-American alliance. Indeed the conception of Britain
as a mediating 'third force' has far more reality in this connection than in its more usual connotation of a half-way house
between U.S.A. and U.S.S.R.

Britain's role in relation to the United States must be to persuade her to lengthen her perspectives in Asia and to think in
terms not of an early war with China but of decades of Asian
development. This in turn would compel an increased respect
for the Indian viewpoint and for economics as against strategy,
and an increased awareness of the historical development of Asia
as against the more ephemeral notion of a defence perimeter in
the Western Pacific.

Britain's prime objective in relation to India should be to help
her to gather internal strength and cohesion. The sooner India
is capable of exerting a really powerful influence in south east
Asia, and is willing to do so, the better for Britain and for world
peace, but this must inevitably wait upon the results of successful economic and political consolidation at home. Britain should
give India all the help she can, and use all her diplomacy to
enlist the help of the United States and others, whether through
the United Nations, the Colombo Plan or by other acceptable
techniques.

How far the situation in Asia is bound to develop towards the
formation of two exclusive blocs, time alone can show. The
policy of China will do more than anything else to determine
the answer. Certainly India, Japan and most of south east Asia
have excellent reasons for rejecting such a prospect, and it was
made amply clear at Bandoeng in April 1955 that they will
struggle to avoid it. So far as the Far East is concerned the dissenting Asian voices at Bandoeng were not of major significance.

Whatever our own assessment of probabilities, we must surely
give full weight to the Asian desire for peaceful co-existence
with China and persuade the Americans to do the same. Any
exercise of western strength in the Far East which threatens to
frustrate this Asian desire is likely to meet increasing resistance,
and to divide rather than unite non-communist Asia. From

F

policies of this kind only the expansionist elements in China, if such there be, could gain.

There can, of course, be no guarantee that Asians, on taking control of their own destinies once again, will make a better job of it than Europeans have made of their continent. What is essential in the formulation of British and western policies, however, is to realise that in the new chapter which is opening, Asian trends of thought will gather strength and that western intervention will be beneficent and effective only in so far as it supplements the underlying Asian trend, and does not seek merely to make Asians instruments of western policy.

POLICY FOR THE COMMONWEALTH

P. C. GORDON WALKER

THE question may well be asked why a chapter on Commonwealth policy figures in a book that is otherwise devoted mainly to immediate questions of foreign policy.

It is true that the essence of the Commonwealth is that its members treat each other on a 'better than foreign' basis. Indeed, perhaps the best definition of the Commonwealth is that its member countries are not foreign one to another. Although each is a distinct and sovereign nation they are all in such a close relationship that they can, if they wish, treat each other in specifically favoured ways that would not be possible were they 'foreign'. This is not only a matter of their attitude towards one another; it is also a matter of international law and practice. Other countries recognise that, since the Members of the Commonwealth together form a political entity, they can confer benefits on each other that need not be extended under most-favoured nation treaties and the like to foreign countries. This is an aspect of the recognition of the Queen as Head of the Commonwealth that is often overlooked—it is the mark by which foreign countries recognise that the Members of the Commonwealth form a close association that has a certain status as such in the comity of nations. In this sense, then, the relations between the United Kingdom and the other Members of the Commonwealth cannot be considered as belonging to its 'foreign policy.'

On the other hand, just because of the size and intimacy of the Commonwealth, the relations between its members form a vital part of 'international affairs'. The total population of the Commonwealth is now over 500 million—about a quarter of the entire population of the world. So close and intimate is the consultation between the members, so far do they take into account each others' views and interests, that their relations constitute perhaps the most significant and effective portion of their foreign policy, considered in the practical rather than the legal sense. Moreover, the effectiveness extends far beyond the confines of the Commonwealth; for each member has close relations with foreign countries outside the Commonwealth and, in conducting these strictly foreign relations, each member is affected by its concern for the views of other Members of the Commonwealth.

It would therefore leave out of account a very large part of Britain's real impact on the world if we were to omit Commonwealth relations from a consideration of our foreign policy. At the same time we cannot study Commonwealth relations in the same way as foreign policy in the ordinary sense. Commonwealth relations are both more intimate and continuous than the normal relations between foreign countries. It is not so much specific decisions that we must consider as the nature of the Commonwealth relationship itself. It is a growing and changing relationship and its effectiveness and impact upon the world depend upon the maintenance and development of the Commonwealth as a unique political association.

We must, of course, give thought to particular questions of foreign policy and to actual difficulties that exist between some of the members. But, if we wish to transform an actual Empire into an actual Commonwealth and to make this actual Commonwealth function to the best effect, we must above all understand the peculiar nature and method of working of the Commonwealth, including its constitutional structure. If Labour is to frame a full and comprehensive foreign policy for Britain we need to do some hard thinking about this neglected aspect of our policy.

Commonwealth relations cannot be made a direct object of party political controversy, because it would be fatal if the Members altered their attitude towards the Commonwealth with every change of government.

Nevertheless Labour should stress much more than it does that it is the true party of Commonwealth. One of our major tasks should be to make our distinctive concept of Commonwealth part of the accepted policy of the country—a policy that Labour will be best fitted to carry out. Both the Labour and Conservative concepts of Commonwealth have a respectable

ancestry that goes back to the very origins of the Commonwealth. Indeed they are both contained in the Durham Report,
which is rightly regarded as the charter of the Commonwealth.
This document is famous for laying down the fundamental
principle of 'Dominion status'. But it also drew a fundamental
distinction between matters of 'Dominion' concern for which
Canada should be solely responsible and matters of 'imperial'
concern for which the United Kingdom should be responsible.

In one form or another this picture of the Commonwealth as
a super-state capable of pursuing a single imperial policy has
underlain the characteristic Conservative concept of Commonwealth. Theoretically the idea could be translated into practice
by central organs in which all members equally shared. One of
the last influential restatements of this idea occurred as late as
1951 in *Britain Strong and Free*, the Conservative election mani-
festo, with its proposals for a 'permanent civil liaison staff', a
'Commonwealth Defence Council' and a 'Combined Staff'. All
such proposals have always been still-born. The Conservatives
found it impossible even to attempt to implement these election
promises. In practice the only way in which the Conservative
desire for a single Commonwealth policy in the fields of defence
and foreign policy could be realised would be by conceding to
Britain the pre-eminent role of the mother country and metropolitan power of the Commonwealth. The Conservative concept of Commonwealth has therefore always borne two characteristics: first, adherence to the symbols of a 'British' Commonwealth—'kith and king', personal loyalty to the Crown as
a test of true membership, the Union Jack. Secondly, resistance
to change and development, for this has always been away from
their ideal. Conservatives have fought a continually losing battle
in the Commonwealth.

Step by step and without deviation, the alternative idea of the
Commonwealth latent in the Durham Report—that of a free
association of sovereign and equal nations—has triumphed. This
is the concept of Commonwealth which is characteristic of the
British Labour Party and which we must thoroughly understand and wholly embrace. Both history and progress are on
our side.

The Report of the Committee of Prime Ministers and Heads

of Delegations to the Imperial Conference of 1926 (sometimes known as the Balfour Declaration), and the Statute of Westminster of 1931, gave the first formal expression to the idea of a Commonwealth of equal and sovereign nations. But their true significance is widely misunderstood.

Contrary to the generally accepted view, their main cause was not simply the growth of the 'Dominions' to adult nationhood. Indeed the opposite is the truth; the Statute of Westminster preceded and anticipated the achievement of this nationhood. In the period 1926–31 no 'Dominion' yet possessed the strength or resources to look after itself in the world. Even the countries that most strongly pressed for a formal statement of equality, assumed that the Royal Navy would continue to guard their security and that the Foreign Office would continue to conduct the foreign policy of the whole Empire. Moreover, the Statute of Westminster was against the strong feelings of the majority of the Commonwealth. Winston Churchill voiced apprehensions that were widespread in Britain; the British in Canada and South Africa were far from happy, while Australia and New Zealand actually insisted on a clause in the Statute exempting them from its provisions. The question that we must ask is—why was so great a change made in the constitutional definition of the Commonwealth when it was both largely formal and so generally opposed? The explanation throws much light on the inherent nature of the Commonwealth which is still working itself out today.

It was Canada (supported by South Africa and Eire) that led the way in pressing for changes against the established and majority view. The basic reason for her attitude to the Commonwealth was that, like these other two countries, Canada had a large non-British population. As the most developed 'Dominion' she had first to face the implications of this fact. On the one hand, she needed to remain in the Commonwealth. The British Canadians were deeply and emotionally committed to the connection, and any attempt to sever it would have split the nation. The French-speaking Canadians also much preferred to be a powerful minority in Canada rather than an insignificant minority amongst many others in the United States. Only by remaining in the Commonwealth could Canada maintain her national unity and her national identity against the tremendous pull of her southern neighbour. (All these factors were absent in Eire, which could thus without difficulty leave the Commonwealth.)

On the other hand, Canada could not accept the traditional concept of a 'British' Commonwealth. Her whole existence as an internally united people depended upon full equality between her British and French-speaking citizens. In a Commonwealth that was 'British', the British Canadians would automatically enjoy a superior status; they would in a subtle but real sense, by the mere fact of their race, belong to the group of true citizens of the Commonwealth, from which French-speaking Canadians would be excluded. It was therefore in order to assert her *internal* rather than her external nationhood that Canada had to insist so early upon a reformulation of the doctrine of Commonwealth. She was impelled to demand formal but premature equality with Britain because this was the only way of rejecting the 'super-state' concept of the Commonwealth, which involved a tacit or open acceptance of the idea of a 'British' Commonwealth.

Two conclusions of prime importance emerge from this view of the Statute of Westminster. First, it created a Commonwealth in which French-speaking Canadians and Afrikaners could live in equality with British communities. This established a pattern of *racial* equality which, although it extended at this time only to European races, established a principle of general application. Secondly, the Statute of Westminster made it clear that there was no way of achieving racial equality except by the assertion of national equality.

Although in 1931 racial equality and internal national unity were more potent than nationalism in the ordinary sense, this factor was also of course already of some significance; refusal to recognise it would have led to internal strains. As time went on, straightforward nationalism became ever more potent, and in due course the actual terms of the Statute of Westminster were, so to speak, retrospectively validated. The changing attitude of Australia well illustrated the dominant role that came to be played by nationalism. Although she vigorously combated the Canadian concept of the Commonwealth, she came to adopt it in fact whilst denying it in words. She was, for instance, the first Commonwealth country to insist on her right to nominate her own Governor General, and perhaps the most dramatic instances of the assertion of sovereign equality in the Commonwealth were her withdrawal of her divisions from the Middle East in the second World War and her later adherence to the ANZUS Pact. During the war both Australia and New Zealand passed legislation to bring themselves within the terms of the Statute of Westminster which they had so strongly opposed twenty years earlier.

Nevertheless the impact of nationalism upon the Commonwealth came largely *after* the Statute of Westminster. Looking back, we can say that already by 1926–31, long before anyone had begun to envisage the future shape and size of the Commonwealth, it had been made clear that in order to exist at all *the Commonwealth had to be both multi-racial and multi-national.* These two attributes were interdependent; by adapting itself to accommodate proud nations, the Commonwealth found room also for proud races.

The advent to power of the Labour Government in 1945 brought a sharp clash between the Labour and Conservative concepts of Commonwealth. The most dramatic of a number of related acts of policy was the recognition of the independence of India, Pakistan, Ceylon and Burma. The Conservatives acquiesced in a deed they would not themselves have done, and therefore with reluctance and regret. They kept up a running criticism of 'Labour's betrayal of the Empire'. Winston Churchill spoke of the 'loss of India'. Disastrous change for the worse in the whole structure of the Commonwealth was foretold. The crowning success of Attlee's policy was the decision by India, Pakistan and Ceylon, contrary to the expectation of the experts, not to take the Burma road but to continue their Membership of the Commonwealth; and the fundamental reason why they did so was that the 'old' Commonwealth had *already* transformed itself into the sort of association into which they could fit easily and naturally.

The existing members could accept the Asian nations as a matter of course because it seemed natural to them and to the British Government that a nation in the Commonwealth should acquire sovereign independence in the same way as they themselves had done. This is the reason why the United Kingdom handled the problem of nationalism in Asia and Africa with so much greater success and foresight than Holland or France, who had never adapted themselves to the acceptance of equality with European colonies before ever the question arose of the equality of non-European colonies. In the case of the United Kingdom a pattern of Commonwealth already existed. At the same time the Asian Members found that it was impossible to be more sovereign than Canada or Australia and that it was as easy for Indians, Pakistanis and Ceylonese to feel at home in the Commonwealth as for Africkaners or French-speaking Canadians.

There was no essential difference between Labour's attitude towards the Membership of the Asian nations and its later unqualified acceptance of the right of Australia and New Zealand to join the ANZUS Pact although Britain was excluded from it. In terms of practical policy there was much to be said for the ANZUS Pact. In the second World War Australia and New Zealand realised that, if the United Kingdom were closely engaged in Europe or the Middle East, the British Navy could not guard their sea-lanes and defend them against invasion. If these two countries were to play any part in Commonwealth strategy and send forces (say) to Singapore, they must be sure that their own back door was bolted against invaders; this only the United States could guarantee. But for some such arrangement as the ANZUS Pact, Australia and New Zealand would have no alternative but to keep their troops at home for their own defence. Whether or not the United Kingdom should be a party to the ANZUS Pact was a question of practical politics. There was a good deal to be said for the ultimate widening of the ANZUS Pact into a broader arrangement including Britain and other countries, and this is one aspect from which we must regard SEATO.

British Conservative opposition to the pact shifted the argument on to false ground. It raised the question of the *right* of Australia and New Zealand to conclude such a pact to the exclusion of Britain. This led Australia to point out with vigour and acerbity that she had equal rights with Britain to pursue her own foreign policy and that there was no difference between

Australia's participation in the ANZUS Pact to the exclusion of the United Kingdom and the participation of the United Kingdom and Canada in NATO to the exclusion of Australia. In both cases, all the Commonwealth countries concerned recognised an over-riding duty to help one another and to keep one another fully informed. In practice Winston Churchill, despite all his criticism in opposition, had quietly to swallow the ANZUS pact when he was in office. Had he been in office earlier our relations with Australia might have been gravely strained.

Great constitutional changes have accompanied the enlargement of the Commonwealth by the addition of the Asian Members. It is commonly implied by Conservatives that these changes have been the *consequence* of the membership of the Asian nations and that they have led to a weakening of the symbols and links of Commonwealth unity which could otherwise have been avoided. Labour is held responsible for an unfortunate and unnecessary loosening of the bonds of Empire. It is true that all these great constitutional changes have made it easier for the Asian Members to remain in the Commonwealth. But they would all have come about in essentially the same form even apart from the Membership of the Asian nations.

Two critical legal changes establish this important truth. One is the question of appeals to the Judicial Committee of the Privy Council. Even had there been no Asian Members of the Commonwealth, the feeling would have arisen that the hearing of appeals by a court sitting in London was in conflict with full national sovereignty. The proof is that Canada and India simultaneously abolished such appeals in 1949, while South Africa and Pakistan did the same in 1950. Ceylon is among the countries that have so far retained appeals to the Privy Council. Unless, perhaps, an itinerant court were established which sits in all parts of the Commonwealth, there can be little doubt that in due course all Members will follow the lead that has been given by the 'old' no less than 'new' members.

The radical change in the legal concept of Commonwealth citizenship provides an even clearer example of changes that have been attributed to the membership of the Asian nations but which would have come about in any case. Originally the status of British subject was defined in terms of common allegiance to the Crown; all British subjects were everywhere the same sort of legal creature with rights and duties that were uniformly defined. Even before the second World War this principle had been infringed in a good many cases. After the war the whole basis of Commonwealth citizenship was changed. Today each Commonwealth country defines its own nationals by its own legislation, and British subjects or Commonwealth citizens (the terms are interchangeable) no longer form a homogeneous legal category with uniform rights and duties all deriving from common allegiance to the Crown. They are merely the aggregate or sum total of all the citizens of Commonwealth countries, who acquire their varying rights and duties from local allegiance to their own country. Each Commonwealth country recognises the citizens of every other as being distinct from aliens and gives them some degree of privilege, although the degree varies very greatly. This is a very considerable change, but it was not in any way due to the membership of the Asian countries. It was in fact Canada that led the way and made the change necessary.

At the end of the war Canada enacted legislation to define her own nationals in terms of local allegiance. This was an inevitable development in a Commonwealth of sovereign nations, and it occurred *before* the independence of India. Britain and all other Commonwealth countries would in any case have had to adapt their legislation to Canada's initiative, whether or not there had been Asian Members of the Commonwealth. The term 'Commonwealth citizen', to which objection is sometimes taken, finds its first legal definition in the Canadian Act to describe the citizens of all other Commonwealth countries.

Even the recognition of a republic in the Commonwealth is by no means so revolutionary a change as appears at first sight. Substantially the same constitutional changes would have had to be made at about the same time and in much the same form, even apart from the membership of India.

The essential constitutional feature of the Commonwealth has always been the dual role of the Crown. On the one hand the Crown has been the symbol of national independence; each realm has achieved sovereignty by self-government in the Queen's name. She must act on the advice of the Ministers in each of her realms in precisely the same manner. At the same time the Crown has also been the symbol of the unity or free association of all the nations of the Commonwealth. These two roles were combined in the Statute of Westminster with its doctrine of 'common allegiance'. But the whole constitutional history of the Commonwealth since 1931 has been towards a complete distinction and separation between the nature of these two roles of the Crown in the Commonwealth. Gradually the Queen's realms have concentrated the entire authority of the Crown into their own hands, until all Commonwealth countries now possess the right to appoint their own ambassadors, to have their own Great Seals, to maintain their own armies and navies, to declare war or to refrain from doing so. The vindication of equality of status with the United Kingdom has meant that the whole sovereignty of the Crown is exhausted and fully used up in its role as the symbol of sovereign independence. In consequence no sovereignty remains inherent in the Crown in its capacity as the symbol of the unity of the Commonwealth. In this role the Crown is not an object of allegiance, but merely a symbol of the will of the Members to remain in the Commonwealth. No authority can be exercised in the Queen's name on behalf of the Commonwealth as a whole; there are no Ministers who can advise her in this capacity. This is the constitutional culmination of the Canadian concept of the Commonwealth, for it removes any constitutional base for the operation of the Commonwealth as a super-state.

This development was complete by the end of the second World War and before the problem of India's membership as a republic had to be faced. The reason why a solution of this problem was so easily found was that no real problem was presented. On the one hand there is no essential difference between a constitutional Governor General, appointed on the advice of the Ministers concerned, and a constitutional President; one can be substituted for the other without disturbing the relationship between the Queen and her realms. On the other hand a republic can accept the Queen as Head of the Commonwealth because no vestige or sovereignty or allegiance vests in this role of the Crown. Thus the incorporation of India in the Commonwealth as a republic only made explicit a constitutional development that was already implicit, and which would in any case have had to be made explicit in some form.

Even if South Africa had not demanded a clearer statement of its right to become a republic, there was pressure for a redefinition of the role of the Crown in the Commonwealth that would have amounted to much the same thing. Once again Canada led the way. In order to emphasise even more clearly her exclusive right to govern herself in the Queen's name, she wanted a change in the royal title that would make the Queen as much Queen of Canada as Queen of the United Kingdom. This change to a 'locally variable title' would have had to be made even had India not become a republic. It was in fact made under a British Conservative government, though all the preparatory work had been done by Labour. Once the locally variable title was adopted, some new royal description would have had to be found that could occur in each of the Queen's local titles to indicate that the Crown was the symbol of the free association of all the Members. This would have been essentially the same problem that India presented, and some description similar to 'Head of the Commonwealth' would have had to be adopted to solve it.

Thus the great constitutional transformation of the Commonwealth that came about whilst Labour was in office was in essence an outward recognition of the changes that had already come about in the relationship between the Members. Historically considered, it was the consummation of the reformulation of the doctrine of Commonwealth started by Canada in the 1926–31 period.

This does not mean, of course, that these changes were inevitable. It needed boldness and imagination to take the initiative in further transforming the Empire into a Commonwealth. Had this step not been taken when it was, the Commonwealth would certainly not have been enlarged by the membership of the Asian nations, and this would have jeopardised the future adherence to the Commonwealth of nations in Africa, the West Indies and elsewhere. Even the 'old' Commonwealth would have been shaken and might even have been diminished in size had the necessary changes been stubbornly help up.

Many Conservatives tend to regard only the 'old' Commonwealth as a natural unit. What has happened, in their eyes, is that a number of 'new' peripheral members have been loosely attached to an inner core of genuine 'foundation' members. Such a view would not only lead to a grave weakening of the Commonwealth; it is also palpably opposed to the actual facts. The Commonwealth, as it exists today and as it is evolving, forms a single and all-inclusive 'natural unit'. It is in no sense a haphazard or artificial grouping of nations, but the product of an historical process that has been at work through all its parts since its inception.

As a matter of history, the whole Commonwealth, 'new' and 'old', is the product of British imperialism—or rather of the propensity of British imperialism to transform itself into its opposite. We wish to change the Empire into a Commonwealth, but had there been no Empire there could be no Commonwealth.

Throughout the Empire British rule implanted certain characteristics and political ways of life, particularly the British type of Parliamentary democracy and rule of law. These characteristics have gone so deep that they have become part of the national being of the countries of the Commonwealth. But this was only possible because these characteristics passed out of British possession into the possession of previously subject peoples and became the main vehicle for independence movements against British rule—movements before which Britain was powerless. The real reason for the incredible peacefulness of struggles for independence within the modern British Empire and for the smoothness of the transfer of power is that Britain in one case after another has encountered its own image. Liberal nationalism has engendered liberal nationalism, and each has tacitly accepted the force of the values they held in common. Mahatma Gandhi was not simply the product of India but of an India that could turn against Britain her own political weapons; he could not have arisen in an India ruled by Stalin or Hitler.

This pattern of self-negating imperialism has applied not only in the case of the Asian countries, and in colonies that are now on their way to final independence; it applied equally in the case of the older Members of the Commonwealth. All of them in the same way acquired the habit of independent parliamentary democracy. In some cases this was the result of the bodily transfer of Britons to their shores, but French-speaking Canadians and Afrikaners learnt parliamentary democracy in the first place as the consequence of British rule and example. In every case independence was achieved by the challenge of native parliamentary democracy to the parliamentary democracy of Britain.

To their common historical experience the countries of the Commonwealth owe the distinguishing feature that marks them off from foreign countries. This is their possession of a unique *capacity to cooperate*. This is so much taken for granted that its importance is widely underrated. It is the precondition of the unity of the Commonwealth.

Various Commonwealth countries have different views about the foundations of democracy. South Africa excludes non-whites from the electorate on principle; Pakistan has declared herself to be a 'Muslim democracy'. These differences are important and present problems for the Commonwealth. It is none the less the fact that every Commonwealth country has a parliamentary government. South Africa works a Cabinet system based on a parliamentary majority, and enjoys a high tradition of independent courts; Pakistan, after careful consideration, decided to reject American presidential democracy in favour of parliamentary government.

Common parliamentary government is one of the major factors of unity in the Commonwealth. It produces in every Commonwealth country 'natural opposite numbers' in a way that is unknown outside the Commonwealth. All Commonwealth Prime Ministers are the same sort of constitutional creature; they all have identical status, rights and duties in their own countries, and they all conceive of Parliament and Cabinet in similar terms. The same thing is true of other Ministers, of civil servants, members of the opposition, judges, lawyers, generals. Commonwealth countries can always meet on the same level and their representatives at all levels speak the same political language.

Granted this unique capacity to cooperate, members have an interest in making the best use of it. Each Commonwealth Government gains by being able to count on the goodwill, understanding and general support of the others, but it can only do so in so far as it is itself willing to take the views and interests of other members into account when framing its own policies.

There is thus a tendency that arises out of the very nature of the Commonwealth for each Member to put the best construction upon the actions of the rest. This natural tendency has been strengthened since the end of the war owing to the vast preponderance of American power. Every Commonwealth country has extremely close relations with the U.S.A.; the United Kingdom, Canada, Australia, New Zealand and Pakistan have military and economic ties, and India counts on American aid for the fulfilment of her economic plan. Friendly relations with the United States amounting in most cases to alliance are essential to the whole Commonwealth. But it is this very closeness with America that brings the Members of the Commonwealth closer to one another. So tremendous is the magnetic attraction of the United States that, if each Commonwealth country were wholly on its own, it would tend to be drawn completely into the American orbit. Only by holding together can they associate in their different ways with the United States on more equal terms.

Principles of Cooperation

Certain general conclusions about the working of the Commonwealth follow from this picture of it as a natural unit, some of which differ sharply from the instinctive Conservative attitude.

First, we must always act in regard to all other Members of the Commonwealth, old and new, present and future, on the principle of 'best construction'. We must ourselves make the interests of other Commonwealth countries part of the basis of our own policy decisions.

Secondly, the idea of a two-tier Commonwealth consisting of first and second class Members must be totally and resolutely rejected. It is not only alien to the fundamental socialist faith in the equal dignity of all nations, but would also be fatal to the Commonwealth. The slightest denial of the full and equal Membership of the Asian nations must also call in question the status of the 'older' Members. The sovereignty of Canada and Australia is every whit as absolute as the sovereignty of India or Pakistan; the racial equality of French-speaking Canadians or

Afrikaners is every whit as absolute as that of Asians in the Commonwealth.

Thirdly, we must regard the Commonwealth as one without a mother country or metropolitan power. This is one of its unique but inescapable features; since all members are equal in status there can be no pre-eminence amongst them. Because the United Kingdom is still the largest power in the Commonwealth, she has special duties, but can have no special rights or status, either tacit or explicit. We have to construct a picture of the Commonwealth that will provide for the smooth transition to the day that is certainly coming when the United Kingdom will no longer be the greatest single power in the Commonwealth. It will be even more important then for Britain that the Commonwealth should be strong, large, united and effective.

Fourthly, we must reject all relics of the idea of a 'British' Commonwealth. The British communities are now in a small minority in the total Commonwealth population of 500 million. But, apart from this, neither Canada, India nor South Africa will tolerate a Commonwealth in which the British arrogate to themselves the right to be identified with the Commonwealth. The Commonwealth must be truly multi-racial and multi-national or it cannot survive at all, either in an enlarged or restricted form.

Fifthly, we must adapt our vocabulary of Commonwealth to its actual nature. We must speak simply of the 'Commonwealth' without the prefix, 'British'. We must drop 'Dominion', which is no less repugnant to Canada and South Africa than to India or Pakistan; the word necessarily implies some distinction of status between the United Kingdom and the other members. We must speak of 'Members of the Commonwealth' or 'Commonwealth countries'.

The Crown

Labour must realise the necessity for a proper constitutional theory of Commonwealth. This cannot be dismissed as legal or academic hair-splitting. A group of sovereign nations, diverse and scattered across the face of the earth, must find some way of expressing and defining their relationship, and this formal expression must correspond to the realities of the relationship.

Moreover, if we are to solve the question of new members, we must have some acceptable way of defining Membership of the Commonwealth.

All this became clear in the very thorough discussion, in which I played some part, concerning India's Membership of the Commonwealth as a republic. The Prime Ministers' Declaration of April 1949 on this question is by far the most significant document in the constitutional history of the Commonwealth.

Countries like Canada and Australia were determined that no change should be made in their own relationship to the Crown. They wished to continue to govern themselves in the King's name and to keep their particular form of parliamentary democracy. They were also resolved to retain the Crown as the symbol of the unity between them as Members of the Commonwealth. In the end the other Commonwealth countries— both those whose sense of personal devotion to the Crown was divided or less strong and those that wished then or later to become republics—came to the same conclusion. One by one possible alternative solutions were examined by the Prime Ministers and rejected. A formal treaty binding together the Members of the Commonwealth would have reduced and rigidified the free and flexible relations between them; it would have made them like foreign countries. A written definition of Membership would have been either so precise that it would have driven the Members apart and tended to make them insist on all sorts of reservations, or so wide and general as to be meaningless and to apply equally to many countries not in the Commonwealth. Moreover, had some Commonwealth countries been linked by the Crown and others by some document, this would have implied a two-tier concept of the Commonwealth.

Not only were all alternatives unacceptable, but the Crown needed only a slightly amplified description to be perfectly adapted to serve as the symbol of Commonwealth unity. As we have seen, the Queen's status as Head of the Commonwealth is an accurate reflection of one aspect of the relationship of *all* Members of the Commonwealth; the realms no less than the republics need a symbol of unity that is without sovereignty or authority and which therefore in no way diminishes their own sovereign independence. The Crown is thus indispensable to the Commonwealth because it is its unwritten constitution. It epitomises the relationship that in fact exists between the Members. It forces nothing, but leaves Commonwealth relations free and flexible.

One constitutional corollary of the highest importance follows from the Queen's Headship of the Commonwealth. By the Declaration of April 1949 the Commonwealth was in effect proclaimed to be one of realms and republics. These have a different relationship of their own towards the Crown, but as regards their relationship one to another as Members of the Commonwealth there is not the slightest legal difference between them.

Another consequence of the Queen's Headship of the Commonwealth particularly concerns Britain. This is that the Queen is no longer in any special or different sense Queen of the United Kingdom. She is equally Queen of all her realms—of Canada or Australia no less than of the United Kingdom; in her capacity as Head of the Commonwealth she has an equal relationship to all Commonwealth countries, including the republics. From this it follows that the Queen will spend a great deal of her time out of the United Kingdom and in other Commonwealth countries, and that she should visit the republics as well as the realms. The timing, frequency and destination of these visits is not under the special control of British Ministers; the advice of other Commonwealth governments is of equal weight and validity. It would also be appropriate that the Queen should be empowered, during any prolonged absence from the United Kingdom, to appoint a Governor General to represent her, just as she does during her absences from her other realms.

Migration

One of the most tenacious relics of the old idea of a 'British' Commonwealth is the common attitude towards migration. This is too often regarded as being wholly a matter of the movement of people from the United Kingdom to the 'White Dominions', and it is widely assumed that this outflow should be on as great a scale as possible. Neither of these propositions can be accepted without question.

The problem of migration within the Commonwealth is now one of great complexity. Migrants from India, Pakistan, West Africa and the British West Indies have begun to enter the United Kingdom on a large and mounting scale. There are large communities of Indian origin in Ceylon, British Guiana, Trinidad, Mauritius, Malaya, South Africa and East Africa. The question of restricting further immigration from India has arisen; it is likely to remain a question even after the African peoples run their own countries. Canada, Australia, New Zealand all restrict in one way or another free immigration from Asian countries in the Commonwealth. The British West Indies restrict immigration from the United Kingdom and from each other. These impediments upon movement within the Commonwealth are related to the wider question of race relations, and I will consider them later in that connection.

Even in regard to the narrower question of the movement of population from Britain, circumstances have greatly changed. Britain now needs her own population. She has a great shortage of manpower; she has indeed herself become a country of immigration. The general position is clear. Britain, too, has the right to national equality within the Commonwealth. There can be no question of an automatic obligation upon her to provide a maximum flow of emigrants regardless of her own interests. Like any other Commonwealth country she is entitled to a migration policy of her own, and she is entitled to vary it from time to time, as did the other Members of the Commonwealth when they suddenly cut off migration from Britain during the slump of 1929.

How far should Britain in fact adopt a migration policy? The problem falls into two parts. First, should she begin to control *immigration* from the Commonwealth, as every other Member does? There is undoubted value in the maintenance of the tradition that all British subjects and Commonwealth citizens can come freely to the United Kingdom and there enjoy full political and civic rights. Britain undoubtedly gains from such a policy, since there is a very valuable counterflow of skilled and professional migrants from other parts of the Commonwealth. Nevertheless the United Kingdom must have the right to control the inflow from other Commonwealth countries. The only absolute condition is that, if the right were ever exercised, it must be applied equally to all Commonwealth countries. There must not be the slightest hint, either in law or in fact, of colour discrimination.

Secondly, should Britain control *emigration* to other parts of the Commonwealth? We need not worry our heads about grandiose schemes of mass-migration. These would not only be flatly against Britain's own interests, but, by reducing Britain to a third-rate power, would fatally weaken the Commonwealth. In any case emigration is by its nature much less amenable to control than immigration. The right of citizens to leave their country is one of the pillars of democracy; so is their right to stay in their own country.

However, some influence can be exercised by propaganda, by facilities offered through Labour Exchanges and by assisted passages. In these matters Britain should henceforth be guided by the following principles (so long as her labour shortage remains):

1. Britain can more easily absorb alien immigrants into her population of 50 million than can Commonwealth countries with far smaller numbers. A certain intake of foreigners and outflow of Britons is therefore reasonable.

2. Any subsidisation of fares should be paid not by Britain but by the receiving country. The United Kingdom now invests a great deal of capital in the education, health and welfare of every child; all the benefit of this investment accrues to the country of immigration.

3. Britain should have some say in the rate of subsidisation of fares and in the type of extent of advertisement by Commonwealth countries seeking to attract migrants. There may be certain categories of skilled workers that Britain needs no less urgently than another Commonwealth country. It is also in Britain's interest that as far as possible there should be a cross-section emigration; not only young skilled workers but their dependents old and young should be taken by the receiving country. There is a good deal to be said for a degree of planned migration, involving (say) the establishment of a factory in some other Commonwealth country accompanied by the movement of workers and

their families. This can never be done on a great scale because many of the workers may prefer to remain in this country. In general Australia has been far more ready than Canada or New Zealand to take a cross-section of British population.

4. By propaganda and other means Britain should try to influence those who wish to emigrate to go to Commonwealth countries rather than to the U.S.A. or elsewhere.

5. It is desirable that Britons should continue to go for their working lives to Commonwealth countries in Asia and Africa in which they may well not wish to settle and become immigrants in the full sense.

On a balance of considerations it seems that Britain can reasonably afford an outflow of migrants averaging about 100,000 a year. Even this figure would involve a significant decrease in population over a generation, which it would not be in Britain's interest to contemplate were she not a Member of the Commonwealth. In practice the rate of migration to the Commonwealth seems to have settled down at around this figure, and this is probably the rate that can be reasonably assumed.

On this assumption, British migration will be able only to make up about half the intake of population by Canada, Australia, New Zealand and South Africa. Their total average rate of immigration is about 200,000 a year—double what Britain can afford to send. All these countries have in fact since the war been taking in at least as many non-British as British migrants. Already the percentage of British in Canada is below 50 per cent; in South Africa it is about one-third of the white population. Australia and New Zealand are not quite so overwhelmingly British as they claim, for they count as British all people born in the country, whatever their parentage; Australia, in particular, has absorbed a considerable number of non-British immigrants since the war, most of them with assisted passages. The course of migration can therefore be expected to emphasise the changes in the nature of the Commonwealth that have already come about. Even if the entry of Asians into white and African countries continues to be restricted, the non-British element in Canada, Australia and New Zealand is certain to increase.

Consultation

Labour must be quite clear about the proper methods for increasing and strenghtening Commonwealth cooperation. Some people deplore the fact that Britain has more elaborately organised relations with NATO or OEEC than with the Commonwealth. But it would be a fatal error to try and transplant to the Commonwealth the machinery of these arrangements and alliances between foreign countries.

In the first place, the Commonwealth cannot be organised as an exclusive bloc. There is a deep feeling running through the Commonwealth (which is just as strong in Canada as in India) against any attempt at 'ganging up' on the rest of the world. All Commonwealth countries, including Britain, value their freedom to associate closely with countries outside the Commonwealth. We must therefore observe the principles of 'non-exclusiveness' in Commonwealth cooperation. This is ultimately a source of strength. Granted that Members of the Commonwealth retain and improve their methods of intimate consultation, the wider their contacts the greater will be their collective influence in the world.

Secondly, Commonwealth unity cannot be created by machinery. The nature of the Commonwealth is such that its unity must come from below; it must spring out of the natural affinity between the Members, out of their capacity and desire to cooperate. We must start from the assumption of a desire to work together. Appropriate machinery may give greater scope to the desire, but it could not create a unity that was not there.

As Mr. MacKenzie King pointed out, Commonwealth consultation is a continuing consultation between cabinets. It is a question of providing for a meeting of minds between governments each of which determines its own policy. The essential problem is to devise ways by which this meeting of minds can occur at a stage before cabinets have gone too far in making policy decisions. Great progress has been made in this direction since the war, particularly under the Labour government. There is now an intricate round-the-clock interchange of telegrams and despatches between Commonwealth capitals. Meetings between Prime Ministers and other Ministers have since 1945 become a regular occurrence.

Further improvements must be made along these established lines. There could, first, be a more organised exchange of views at the official level. One of the advantages of the Commonwealth is that civil servants have the same function in every country. They advise Ministers and prepare policy, but never make policy themselves. If there could be more regular and permanent interchange between Commonwealth civil servants, this would mean that Commonwealth cabinets would approach their policy decisions better informed about the thinking of their partners; they would decide policy against a background of agreed facts and figures.

Secondly, we should be prepared to run greater security risks in the imparting of information to other Commonwealth countries. There are, of course, secrets that can only be divulged in the narrowest circles, but too much stress on security can do great harm to the major objective of Commonwealth cooperation. Britain should, in particular, take a firmer line about the passing on of secrets shared with the United States, some of which are of British origin. So close is British cooperation with America that the American preoccupation with security can gradually extinguish whole fields of information that should pass freely to other Commonwealth countries. Nor should we allow the United States to force us into security-discrimination between different Commonwealth countries.

In general, we must cherish the basic idea that the relationship between Commonwealth countries is 'better than foreign'. It rests on the assumption of willing cooperation such as cannot be counted on between foreign countries. Alliances and treaties between foreign countries extend commitments by defining them. But definition of commitments between Commonwealth countries must limit and diminish them. We should rejoice that there is neither need nor possibility of a NATO or OEEC between Commonwealth countries.

India and South Africa

The need to put the best construction upon the actions of other Members of the Commonwealth raises problems of special difficulty when there is any great divergence between our own basic policies and those of any other Member. Such problems arise in connection with India and South Africa.

Our Commonwealth relationship with India is affected by two main considerations. First, India is in sharp dispute with Pakistan over Kashmir, and with South Africa (and to a certain degree with Ceylon) over the status of people of Indian origin. This raises the general question of disputes within the Commonwealth.

Serious disputes inevitably weaken the texture of the Commonwealth. But it would be an even graver violation of the nature of the Commonwealth to attempt to set up any machinery for the compulsory settlement of disputes. This would be to commit the cardinal error of trying to impose unity by machinery. Sovereign nations cannot be compelled to accept arbitration.

Disputes between Members also raise difficulties for the other Members. Should Britain take sides over Kashmir or join in condemnation of South Africa at the United Nations?

If we are to have a Commonwealth policy, we cannot consider such matters solely on their merits, as we would were the countries concerned foreign countries. We cannot apply the doctrine of best construction partially and with discrimination; if we depart from it at all, the principle itself will be endangered and Commonwealth cooperation will suffer. Where there are disputes, other members can only follow the principle of best construction by remaining neutral.

Our relations with India are effected, in the second place, by the neutralist foreign policy which distinguishes her from all other Commonwealth countries, including the other Asian Members. There is also the consideration that the United States tends to apply to India the principle that those who are not with us are against us. We must refuse to be parties to such an attitude towards India. It should be a cardinal point of British policy to cooperate as closely as possible with all the Asian Members. Both our own influence and that of the whole Commonwealth depends upon the maintenance of a bridge of intimate friendship between Asia and the west. It is one of the unique advantages of the Commonwealth that it contains within itself the only such bridge.

We must apply the principle of best construction in regard to

India as well as to Pakistan and Ceylon. We must recognise that Indian neutralism is a distinctive and positive policy. It is not, like other forms of neutralism, based on either fear or indifference. It does indeed presuppose a balance of power between democracy and communism in the world; if Britain, for instance, were to adopt India's policy of non-involvement, this would cause such a shift of power in the world that India herself would at once be in danger and might have to reconsider her policy. But India's neutralism is not a disguised form of communism. India is democratic and strongly opposed to her own internal communists. She would be equally opposed to communist aggression in south east Asia. At the same time India's neutralism is based on a firm realisation that the only way of defeating communism in Asia is to set the force of nationalism against it. This is a truth that the west is too often apt to forget. There is no concealing the divergence of foreign policy between India and ourselves, but just as we can count on India regarding our policy as honest and sincere, so must we accept that India's policy is one that can be pursued by men of democratic integrity.

Relations with South Africa raise even more acute problems and therefore demand the utmost clarity of thought. The essence of the problem is that in this case the twin principles of the Commonwealth are in conflict. South Africa's race policy not only conflicts with the principle of racial equality which is fundamental to the Commonwealth; it also conflicts with the policy of the United Kingdom, the other Commonwealth power in Africa. On the other hand, South Africa claims to be asserting in her own internal affairs the principle of national equality, which is no less fundamental to the Commonwealth.

There are many who say that the principles of socialism demand that we should think only of racial equality, and this is certainly so in regard to our own policies. Some even demand that 'we should throw South Africa out of the Commonwealth'. But if British socialism includes amongst its principles belief in the Commonwealth, we must be careful what we are about.

First, we must not fall into the imperialist error of thinking that the United Kingdom still runs the Commonwealth and that it can decide who shall or shall not be Members. This is now a question for all Members equally. The question, then, must be put this way: should the Commonwealth as a whole 'expel' South Africa?

In this connection we must remember that South Africa represents in an extreme form a problem of race-relations that is by no means limited to South Africa. As we have seen, most Commonwealth countries except the United Kingdom discriminate in some degree between races in their immigration policy. It can be argued with force that no country can be held to be under a moral obligation to import a race problem where none yet exists, and that therefore a discriminatory immigration policy can be justified. But even when we come to the question of internal discrimination against a race, we find that South Africa is not alone. The Indian Government maintains that Ceylon is discriminating as regards electoral rights against its 'Indian Tamil' population. India, moreover, is far from solving its own problem of untouchability and denies full political rights to certain tribal areas that have never yet been brought under close administration. There is also race discrimination in some of Britain's African colonies and in the Rhodesian Federation. The aboriginal people in Australia are far from enjoying full equality of rights. Even in New Zealand the Maori vote in separate communal electorates.

The problem is far more radical and absolute in South Africa than elsewhere, but any attempt to 'solve' the South African problem by drastic Commonwealth action would raise up difficult problems in many other parts of the Commonwealth— problems that will, like untouchability in India, be best solved if left to time. Moreover, the practice of settling Commonwealth differences by 'expulsion' is one that could spread; Pakistan, for instance, might demand the expulsion of India for what it regards as its crime against democracy in Kashmir.

There is also the consideration that South Africa's policies would certainly not be improved by her exit from the Commonwealth. The Asian countries resolved with their eyes open to remain in a Commonwealth that contains South Africa. If there is any international environment that can induce a change of heart in South Africa it is a Commonwealth whose basic principle is multi-racialism. Were South Africa outside the Commonwealth it would not adopt the policy of 'co-existence' with the Gold Coast and other African states that has recently been enunciated by Mr. Strydom.

One further consideration that is commonly overlooked applies particularly to Britain. So long as the gulf subsists between British and South African native policy, it must be our aim to keep the three territories of Bechuanaland, Basutoland and Swaziland under British administration; this is the spirit and intent of the British South Africa Act of 1909. But British administration of the High Commission Territories depends upon a degree of South African cooperation. That is the fact, whether we like it or not. We cannot reach these territories without passing through or over the Union; their revenue is a percentage of South African customs revenue; and their chief markets and sources of supply lie in South Africa. The main reason why Britain can count on the necessary degree of cooperation from South Africa is the mutual Membership of the two countries in the Commonwealth, from which both derive considerable advantages that are too important to jeopardise. Were South Africa outside the Commonwealth these factors would largely cease to apply and the High Commission Territories with a million African inhabitants might well pass from Britain to South African rule.

On balance, the conclusion is inescapable that we should not contemplate the rupture of the fabric of the Commonwealth. Our policy should be to concentrate on demonstrating the superiority of our own policies in Africa over those of the Union.

Economic Planning

It is perhaps in the economic field that the contrast between Labour and Conservative policy for the Commonwealth is most strikingly demonstrable.

Conservatives and some others cling to the idea of imperial preference, which seems to them to be related to the concept of a unified Commonwealth. Indeed, at the beginning of the century, a tariff-union was regarded as the first step towards political union, on the model of Bismarck's *Zollverein*. Partly for this very reason, and partly because an important part of the trade of every Member lies outside the Commonwealth, the other countries are against an extension of imperial preference; they are, however, prepared to continue the present level of Commonwealth preference, which is not of very great importance, but might be of value if a world slump should occur. The present Conservative government made a sustained effort in 1951 to secure an extension of imperial preference, and was publicly snubbed by the other Members.

The relative unimportance of imperial preference does not mean that we should disregard the need to stimulate and develop the economy of the Commonwealth. On the contrary, this is a vital part of any constructive Commonwealth policy.

The Sterling area is not coterminous with the Commonwealth. It is of comparatively slight importance that some non-Commonwealth countries are included within it. But the fact that Canada is outside is of great significance. No Commonwealth economic policy can be complete that does not aim at bridging the economic gulf that separates Canada from the sterling Commonwealth. We should pursue with far more vigour the investment of every dollar we can spare—whether Canadian or United States dollars—in Canada's rapidly expanding economy. But to achieve this we must be much more careful about the expenditure on other things of dollars that might be invested in Canada. This would, however, involve the use of powers of discrimination of which we have under a Conservative government deprived ourselves.

In the main a Commonwealth economic policy must concentrate upon the development of Commonwealth sterling production. It is vitally important, as countries like Malaya become independent, that the sterling area should work as a voluntary cooperative undertaking. If Malaya were to leave the sterling area the loss of dollars would have catastrophic effects not only upon Britain but upon every other part of the Commonwealth, including India. One of the main cohesive factors in the sterling area is the availability of the British capital market and of the British home market to Commonwealth producers of primary products. If the sterling area is to operate freely and efficiently Britain must make more capital available to the Commonwealth and guarantee a place in its home market for Commonwealth producers. The Conservatives are deterred by reasons of economic doctrine both from directing capital investment and from

using such modern methods as long-term bulk-purchase agreements. This would involve measures of concerted planning and,
above all, a degree of planning in the British home market that
Conservatives will not stomach. Long-term agreements cannot
be fitted into a completely free home market, and that is why
the Conservative Government has torn up practically every
Commonwealth trade agreement concluded by the previous
Labour Government.

Encouragement of Commonwealth production, if it is to
mean anything at all, must mean its encouragement to a point
beyond what it would naturally reach if left to the free play of
the market. In other words some degree of deliberate economic
planning is necessary. Labour has in this connection the immense advantage over the Conservatives of being eager to use
economic planning where it is in the general interest. Labour
will readily collaborate with other Commonwealth governments for the planned encouragement of Commonwealth trade;
it will be prepared to use quotas and other necessary devices,
and can easily fit long-term agreements for the purchase of
staple foodstuffs into its policy for domestic agriculture and
marketing.

Future shape of the Commonwealth

The Labour concept of Commonwealth, because it is based
upon an historical understanding of the Commonwealth, can
be projected with some confidence into the future. The shape
and size of the Commonwealth that is coming into being can be
determined within fairly narrow limits. New Members will be
limited to countries of a certain size that are still colonies in the
British Empire.

On the one hand, foreign countries cannot 'join' the Commonwealth, despite occasional talk to that effect. The Commonwealth is not an artificial creation nor a club that can be
joined; it is a 'natural unit' and therefore has natural limits. It is
made up of countries that have, for historical reasons, certain
profound affinities one with another. Without the will and capacity to cooperate that spring from these affinities, the links of
Commonwealth would become so vague and general as to be
meaningless. It would not be enough, as is sometimes assumed,

for a foreign country to have close natural links with Britain alone; to be a Member of the Commonwealth it would need to have similar affinities with India, Canada, Australia and all the other existing and future Members of the Commonwealth. With the possible exception of the United States, there is no foreign country that comes into this category. It is theoretically conceivable that countries like Israel or the Sudan or Burma that have had a close historical association with the British Empire might become Members, but it is very doubtful whether the bond of unity, once it has been snapped, can ever be restored.

Potential new Members are therefore limited to countries in the Commonwealth that are on the way to independence. But amongst these are very small territories that cannot become full Members because they cannot become nations able to look after their own defence and foreign policy. To take part in the meetings of Commonwealth Prime Ministers, a country must be in a position to undertake the responsibilities of sovereignty.

The proposals to integrate Malta with the United Kingdom (whether or not they are immediately implemented) make it all the more necessary to work out a new solution for the small territories. Most if not all of the remaining small territories do not want the 'Malta solution' but wish to run their own affairs. But what has been suggested for Malta makes them all the more clamant for an equally radical and complete solution to their own problem. It should be our policy wherever possible to encourage small territories to federate into units sufficiently large to take their place as full nation-states of the Commonwealth. Federation should not, however, be rushed; artificial federations may easily fall apart.

In any case there will be a number of small territories that cannot or do not wish to fit into any federation. What should be our policy towards them? As I see it, there is no alternative but the simple solution that has always applied in the Commonwealth—namely complete and unlimited independence. All ideas of a *permanent* reservation to the United Kingdom of defence and foreign policy—however this may be dressed up in honorific trappings—breaks down on the fact that incomplete independence can never be a final resting place. There will always be a demand for full freedom; there will always be an opposition that denounces the local government as a stooge. In countries like Singapore where there is a large subversive communist element this may be a standing danger to order and good government.

The only solution is the recognition in due course of Dominion status in terms of the Statute of Westminster—that is to say, the formal grant of autonomy in all affairs both internal and external. As I have pointed out above, at the time of the Statute of Westminster the then 'dominions' were not yet in fact full nations. They relied on the United Kingdom for the conduct of defence and foreign policy. And they freely made agreements for the use of bases and other facilities. Since then these 'Dominions' have become nations fully capable of looking after all their own affairs. They have in effect left behind 'Dominion status' and the term can no longer be used to describe them. But the term and status that they have vacated have eager new tenants. Mr. Marshall of Singapore and other leaders of the city and island states of the Commonwealth express their aspiration as the achievement of Dominion status.

Labour should declare its intention, as each small territory reaches the stage of fully responsible self-government, to offer it full and complete Dominion status. We would thereby forego the legal right to conduct defence and foreign policy on their behalf, but this is a right that can never in the end be enforced even in regard to quite small territories if they do not wish to concede it—as has been shown by Cyprus and Israel. In exchange for an unenforceable legal right we could count on the sort of goodwill that prevailed in the Commonwealth of 1931. The small territories would not in fact be able to undertake their own defence and foreign policy; some country or other would have to help them. As autonomous Dominions they would be much more likely freely to enter into agreements about any bases that would be mutually advantageous and to concur in their international representation by the United Kingdom Foreign Office.

One advantage of this solution would be that it would be left open whether any particular new Dominion in fact developed, either by federation or by natural growth, into a nation-state that could undertake the full responsibilities of a Member of the

Commonwealth. No embarrassing question of legal status would arise because the Dominion would be autonomous. It would be a question of fact to be settled according to the views of the Dominion itself and the collective judgment of the Commonwealth Prime Ministers. The Colonial Office should be re-christened as the 'Dominions Office'.

There is therefore a limited number of potential new full Members of the Commonwealth—countries in the Colonial Empire that are of sufficient size to be nations. The exact number is indeterminate because it depends upon three unknown factors. The first is where the Commonwealth Prime Ministers will in practice draw the line between large and small territories. The second is the degree to which federations of small territories are formed. The third is the willingness of larger territories who achieve independence to continue as Members of the Commonwealth. It seems highly probably that the lead given by the Asian members will in fact be followed. No difficulties are to be expected from within the Commonwealth. If the United Kingdom sponsors as potential new members territories that are palpably independent and capable of starting on a career as full nations, the remaining members of the Commonwealth will almost certainly concur. South Africa has recently indicated that it is abandoning the implied threat of attempted veto against the membership of Nigeria and the Gold Coast.

We can therefore count on the addition to the existing eight full members of Nigeria, the Gold Coast, the Caribbean Federation, Malaya and the Rhodesian Federation. We can also hope that an East African Federation will be formed after the constituent states have achieved a full democratic franchise. Buganda may well seek to hold out, in which case it can hope to be one of the new Dominions. It is also possible that a Federation of Malaya, Singapore, Sarawak, North Borneo and Brunei may one day be formed.

The Commonwealth in its ultimate shape will consist of some fourteen or fifteen full nation-states whose Prime Ministers attend the meetings of Commonwealth Prime Ministers. In addition there will be a dozen or more new Dominions. The Commonwealth will be one of realms and republics. It is hard to foresee how many members will in due course become

G

republics; it seems probable however, that there will be a considerable majority of realms.

The ultimate difference between the Labour and Conservative concepts of Commonwealth is that Labour looks eagerly forward to the evolution of the Commonwealth in its final form. Its whole policy will be directed towards this consummation.

The Commonwealth, as Labour foresees it, will still for a time have some internal difficulties, but it will be the greatest force for peace and international understanding in the world. Its members will be found in every continent; it will embrace every major religion and race. It will be able to adapt itself smoothly to shifts of power within itself, as other members grow to be greater powers than the United Kingdom itself. In the end the Commonwealth will contain some of the most powerful, prosperous and populous nations in the world.

VII

BEYOND POWER POLITICS

DENIS HEALEY

IT would be foolish to deny that modern diplomatic habits have disadvantages compared with those of the past. Negotiation in private between professionals trained in the art is more likely to settle differences than public debate between politicians. Ideological pharisaism can be a greater obstacle to agreement than cool self-interest. But there is a real danger that the reaction against some obvious defects of modern diplomacy may throw out the baby with the bathwater. In the United States writers like Morgenthau, Kennan, and Lippman have done valuable work in criticising some of the Utopian illusions which distort the formation of American foreign policy. But in leaving national interest as the only standard of diplomatic judgment they risk playing Nietzsche to some Hoosier Hitler. Similarly in Britain conservative pessimists like Butterfield conspire with radical iconoclasts like Taylor to present the traditional anarchy of power politics as at least the best of all possible worlds. An extraordinarily wide range of intellectual opinion seems to have settled on a recipe for world peace closely analagous with the classical Conservative recipe for social peace—self-interest mitigated by charity—in this case, nationalism flavoured by help to the under-developed areas.

Nationalism is certainly the strongest single force in world affairs, and physical power still the ultimate sanction. But nostalgia for the Old Diplomacy cannot help to solve the problems of power politics in a democratic world. Most of the recent innovations in diplomatic practice are the inevitable consequence of political democracy. As American writers have seen more clearly than British, once public opinion can exert a direct influence on the processes of government, it must rule out certain types of diplomatic method no less than it excludes certain types of economic and social development.

The diplomatic reconciliation of conflicting state interests was a comparatively simple task in the eighteenth century. In those days state power was vested exclusively in a narrow ruling class whose culture was often international rather than national, and whose interests were not deeply engaged in relations between their state and others. Diplomatists of goodwill had usually both the time and the authority to compose differences between the governments they represented.

Universal suffrage and the industrial revolution have transformed this situation. Modern diplomatists have to deal with the immediate and vital interests of whole peoples. They have to work under the fitful stare of a public opinion which is rarely well informed even when it is most concerned. They have neither the time nor the authority for that delicate manipulation of the balance of power which the eighteenth century is said to have brought to a fine art.

The mechanistic view of international relations purely in terms of power simply fails to correspond with the way peoples conceive their interests and their rights. The rapid shifts of alliance required to maintain a balance of power have become impossible for a democracy except in war. Even the distinction between the roles of great and small powers, which was fundamental to the rules of the Old Diplomacy, is rejected by democratic opinion. Nationalism itself is one aspect of democracy in action; the concept of the equal rights of nations contradicts the very basis of power politics.

If it is true that democracy on a world scale is incompatible with the traditional international polity of power politics, it is equally true that democracy will dig its own grave unless it can find an alternative polity which is compatible with the special limitations it imposes on diplomacy. It has often been noted that even in a single state democracy cannot survive without a certain level of administrative competence and social responsibility. Similarly a world of democratic nation states is doomed to destruction unless it can substitute a minimum of international order for the anarchy of the past. For, besides the growth of democratic nationalism, many other changes in the last two centuries have destroyed whatever hopes of stability the Old Diplomacy may have offered.

By vastly shrinking space and time and immensely increasing physical power, science has robbed diplomacy of that flexibility it requires for manoeuvre.

Under the Old Diplomacy, when Europe was the centre of the world, dangerous conflicts could often be avoided if a state's interests could be diverted into expansion overseas. Today imperialism is in retreat and there are no unclaimed territories left to conquer. Every continent is crowded with nation states, and even the smallest state today disposes of more physical power than the greatest two hundred years ago. This staggering increase in the power available to nation states has made their conflicts ever more catastrophic. Within a generation there may well be thirty states, each armed with more destructive weapons than any that exist at present. Yet even today, when only three states possess atomic weapons, many scientists believe that war between them might destroy the human race.

Economic changes complicate the problem still further. The demands of an industrial world economy create new diplomatic difficulties which would have daunted Talleyrand or Metternich, and which grow even more terrifying with the colossal growth in Asian populations. Both of today's greatest powers, the U.S.A. and U.S.S.R., industrialised their continents under exceptionally favourable circumstances, with a lasting excess of raw materials over manpower. The nascent super-powers of India and China start with an appalling weight of over-population. Japan's recent history should give warning of the tensions which are liable to ensue.

These are only a few of the factors which prohibit a return to the international polity in which independent nation states seek the best of all possible worlds by the diplomatic exercise of power in the intelligent pursuit of their selfish interests. But there is another factor which would be decisive even by itself. Over nearly a third of the world's surface communist governments are constructing a new international polity which offers one answer to the problems presented by the twentieth century. Yet the communist answer denies all the traditions of liberal democracy. It means transferring the power of nation states into the hands of totalitarian parties which accept the authority of a single centre in Moscow. Whether or how the Soviet

international polity can survive the existence of an independent
Communist Party controlling a country the size of China is still
uncertain. What is certain is that so long as the communist camp
maintains its present solidarity it will take advantage of divisions
outside its frontiers in order to expand. It would be fatal to
underestimate the real grounds which go to justify the confidence of men like Khrushchev and Bulganin that the non-
communist world will disintegrate under the pressure of its own
internal contradictions. If the non-communist countries fail to
control their own internal conflicts they will pay a terrible price
in terms of freedom even if they manage to escape nuclear annihilation.

Thus all the particular problems exercising the democracies
dwindle into insignificance beneath the decisive general challenge—can they, without sacrificing the essentials of their way
of life, construct out of the present anarchy of independent
nation states an international society, which however rudimen-
tary, at least gives hope of avoiding a major catastrophe and
of providing foundations on which future generations may
build?

It is a challenge which should be particularly congenial to
Socialists, whose faith is based on the brotherhood of man. Indeed a generation past it would have been accepted with enthusiasm throughout the Labour Movement. But there is an
element of truth in the gibe that the socialisation of the nation
may mean the nationalisation of socialism. Too often today a
Labour Party conference will greet the demand for an independent foreign policy with frenzied cheers, while it hears an
explanation of the sacrifices and compromises required for a
collective effort in mutinous silence. Utopian myths and parochial interests still tend to distort many Socialists' approach to
world affairs. There is a crying need for modern Fabians to do
for foreign policy what their predecessors did for domestic policy—to examine the facts of the modern world with relentless
and painstaking care in the light of their general principles. Only
thus is it possible to form a rational plan of action. This essay is
intended as a contribution to the groundwork for such a study
—what the eighteenth century might have called a prolego-
menon to a methodology of international politics.

Stated broadly, the problem is to establish a collective influence over the use which states may make of their power, sufficient at least to exclude war as an instrument of policy, to maintain solidarity against external pressure, and to permit a stable and expanding international economy. The methods chosen must be compatible with the existing diversity of social and economic systems outside the communist bloc—and in particular with the special limitations and opportunities presented by political democracy. For the time being at least, it is unrealistic to expect the cooperation of communist states in such an effort, since their leaders have reaffirmed their conviction that lasting international unity cannot be achieved except by governments which accept the major premises of Sino-Soviet communism.

We must start by analysing some of the effects which political democracy has had on the nature of power in international relations. Physical strength, measured in military and economic terms, is in one sense the ultimate source of all international power. But to the extent that public opinion influences foreign policy, the impact of physical power is profoundly influenced by factors which are not physical. Napoleon's military dictum that the moral is to the physical as ten to one is equally true of diplomacy. Much more physical power is required to impose a policy which those concerned feel to be unjust than to support one which has general consent. The distinction between force and consent is fundamental to the democratic pursuit of world order.

It may be said that there are three main types of approach to an international society, those of the engineer, the lawyer and the gardener. The engineer's approach requires that human beings be treated as passive objects for mechanical manipulation by governments; it is represented best by the polity of the communist bloc, and it would be foolish to deny its efficiency. But it depends on compulsion by physical force to a degree which democratic societies would fight to avoid. The lawyer's approach, on the other hand, though it has its place in the democratic world, tends to regard human beings as both more rational and more moral than they are in their international behaviour. It underestimates the relevance of physical force in international politics, and oversimplifies the complexity of interests and motives on which consent depends. The most appropriate approach is normally that of the gardener, who deals with forms of organic life which are not fully subject to either rational or mechanical control. He must understand and accept in advance the limitations set by his materials—and is at all times prepared for the unpredictable.

Fortunately the increasing impact of public opinion on foreign policy in the democratic countries opens new possibilities of achieving world order by consent. In the present era organs of international public opinion play an important role in world politics even when they dispose of no physical power themselves. Not only the United Nations, but such bodies as the Bandoeng Conference, the Arab League or the Council of Europe may exert a major influence by changing public attitudes. Even in this field, however, physical power plays its part. For example, though in Asia Britain has a greater influence than the more powerful United States, because external power is resented, Thakin Nu, despite his exceptional moral qualities, has less influence than Mao Tse Tung or Pandit Nehru, because within the region political influence has a direct relation to national power.

The development of international public opinion is in itself an asset in the effort to build an international society. However inconvenient the impact of public opinion may be in particular cases, it is wholly fortunate that there is an overwhelming weight of public opinion in all states which favours the establishment of some order in the international anarchy. This fact sets real limits to the freedom of national governments in pursuing selfish ends. At no time since the United Nations was founded has any national delegation attacked its purposes as defined in the Charter. And in the few cases where a delegation has boycotted discussions in the Assembly, it has felt it necessary to justify its action in terms of the Charter itself, and has been under pressure in its own country to return as soon as possible—Russia is of course the exception which proves the rule. Even the Soviet Government has to take account of public opinion outside its boundaries, though it is never under similar pressure from its own people. The need to win friends among the emergent uncommitted peoples is one of the main reasons for the change in Soviet policy since Stalin.

Fear of a third world war has been the main stimulus behind this popular support for the United Nations. But there has developed also a positive sense of the human community in which even self-interest plays only a minor role. Professor Toynbee has rightly said that one of the most striking phenomena of this century is the general assumption that the welfare of mankind as a whole is a proper and practicable aim of political action. It is true enough that the strength of this feeling tends to fade dramatically when specific sacrifices are demanded in its name. Nevertheless the fact that it is there at all is important. And the work of bodies like the United Nations International Children's Emergency Fund testifies to its real if limited effect.

In general the establishment of a democratic international order requires a transition from physical force to public consent as the basis of power in world affairs, just as a democratic national order requires that decisions be taken by ballots rather than bullets, by counting heads rather than breaking them. But the process for effecting this transition is extraordinarily complex and difficult. The typical weakness of the juridical approach is over-reliance on the ability of formal agreements to alter behaviour which is rooted in facts of power or facts of opinion. In international affairs law is likely to determine the action of nations only when it expresses the existing pattern of power and reflects the existing climate of opinion. If power is too unevenly distributed, international law tends to be effective only so long as it represents the interests of the stronger countries, and in this case it is unacceptable to opinion in the weaker. So there must be a redistribution of national power in favour of the weaker states before it is possible to organise a transfer of power from national states to some collective international authority.

Though this problem is most evident in the United Nations, because it represents a juridical approach to world order, those who drafted the Charter had learnt much from the history of the League of Nations. In its security organisation they recognised the facts of power in 1945 by giving the victorious survivors of the second World War permanent seats on the Security Council with the right of veto. But their successors have been

dangerously slow to admit later changes in world power relations. There is an overwhelming case for giving India and perhaps Japan permanent seats on the Security Council. Germany's
absence can be excused only by the problems arising from her
present division, while the effective absence of China has no
excuse whatever.

Nevertheless the juridical bias of the United Nations is evident, even in its provisions for maintaining the peace. It treats
military aggression as the one great international crime and
assumes that in any case of war a jury composed of eleven government representatives will be able to fix the responsibility on
one side; and that it is then the duty of all members of the
United Nations to aid the declared victim of aggression.

The difficulties presented by these assumptions are much more
obvious now than they were thirty years ago. In the first place
responsibility for aggression may well be difficult to fix, particularly in a war arising out of frontier incidents. In the second
place, the Security Council consists of governments which have
their own friends and enemies among other governments—
their impartiality cannot be taken for granted. Indeed the Security Council is bound to mirror all the conflicts of power politics
in which its members are engaged; and there is no merit in dis-
guising vulgar conflicts of national interest as conflicts of good
and evil. Finally, in the absence of a supranational authority,
there is nothing to compel the members of the United Nations
to take action against an aggressor when the Security Council
has named him. And if they do, there is the danger that they are
simply turning a small war into a big war—or even into a global
war.

To these technical criticisms must be added the fundamental
one which is made by all communists in theory and by many
others in practice—the belief that some wars are just, and that
since aggression is not always a moral sin it should not be treated
as a political crime. The latest edition of the Soviet Encyclo-
pedia lists as 'just' wars not only wars of defence but also wars
for 'the liberation of colonies and dependent countries from the
oppression of imperialists' and 'the liberation of a people from
the slavery of capitalism'. Some people who were not communists used this argument to justify aggression by North Korea.

Many Americans applied a version of the same principles to their own intervention in Guatemala. And belief that 'preventive wars' are justified is widespread in many countries.

Tempting though this type of argument may be, reflection must show that it is quite incompatible with any attempt to build a world order, and presents the gravest dangers for world peace. Even the communist countries have admitted that it holds dangers for them. China has included among the Five Principles which guide her present foreign policy 'mutual respect for territorial integrity and sovereignty, non-aggression, and non-interference in each others' internal affairs'. Russia seems anxious to make non-aggression pacts with individual non-communist powers, though this of course would be unnecessary if she took seriously her signature of the United Nations Charter.

The fact is that war today presents so immediate a threat to mankind as a whole that it is in the interest of all countries to exclude it as an instrument of policy. This fact helps to answer the specific objections to the United Nations provisions for collective security. Though some types of aggression may slip through the net of legal definition, the more dangerous types are easily identified through the crossing of frontiers with large armed forces. Though certain powers have a large and fairly consistent team of voters in the United Nations, the admission of sixteen new members in 1955 made it more likely that a majority decision would be taken impartially on any major issue.

As for the argument that collective security means turning small wars into large wars, this is true—and therein lies the deterrent. It seems highly probable that the United Nations' action in Korea did deter Russia from promoting other satellite aggressions—particularly against Yugoslavia. And Korea also shows that a war may remain localised in space even when it is internationalised in politics. By putting almost unlimited resources behind the victim of aggression, the United Nations may be able to halt the aggressor without extending the area of the fighting. Its proved readiness to do this would by far be the best deterrent against the local or limited wars which are probably the most dangerous threat to peace in the era of atomic stalemate. For this reason there is a strong case for reviving the attempt to reach agreement on some form of 'international police force'.

The crucial weakness of the United Nations lies of course in the Security Council veto. But though the ability of some great powers to veto action, and of all powers to abstain from action, does reduce the value of United Nations decisions, it does not nullify them. The fact that the United Nations cannot always do everything it was set up for is no argument against it continuing to do what it can. Indeed the veto is an inevitable—and indeed desirable—consequence of the present distribution of international power. Without it, the risk that collective security might push mankind into an unnecessary and undesired global catastrophe would discourage any attempt to use the U.N. machinery for maintaining peace.

Nevertheless, many critics of the United Nations see the fact that its members retain full national sovereignty as completely destroying its value. They believe that progress towards a world order can be made only if states are prepared to surrender sovereignty by treaty to a supranational authority. Some indeed carry the juridical approach to extreme lengths in claiming that 'world government' is a possible solution to our difficulties. But even these enthusiasts find it impossible to agree on the basis by which existing states should be represented in such a world government. Professor Niebuhr tells a story of the World Republic Convention in October 1948 at which an American delegate proposed a system of weighted votes in favour of nations with high literacy and abundance of raw materials and industrial production. An Asian delegate sitting two places to his left immediately protested that weighted representation was immoral.

Such difficulties may be much less daunting if federation is considered among a limited group of nations with a similar culture and social organisation. Many sophisticated politicians have seen federation as the best or only answer to the problems of western Europe since the war. The experience of the European movement provides a case-history in the juridical approach to international order.

At first sight, the prospects for West European federation looked exceptionally bright in 1946. The war itself had destroyed many of the vested national interests which might have been expected to obstruct surrender of sovereignty. Soviet pressure in the east provided a powerful incentive to sink national differences. American predominance in the west created a general desire to achieve continental independence. The Americans themselves, believing that Europe's survival depended on her copying their example, offered high rewards for progress towards federation. Finally, the foreign policy of all three great continental powers was directed for years by Catholic statesmen whose personal desire for federation was fully shared by the Vatican.

The first steps towards a merger of sovereignties were not encouraging. The attempt of the Low Countries to create the Benelux Customs Union, after a good start, soon bogged down in a maze of technical discussions. The Franco-Italian Customs Union sank without trace at the first scream from enraged winegrowers. Realising that public opinion would not swallow an immediate and total fusion of sovereignties, the continental governments decided to seek federation on the instalment plan, by creating a series of supranational authorities to control specific functions of government. The first of these authorities, the socalled Schuman Plan for a Coal and Steel Pool, after a difficult birth, has made slow but steady progress. But the long agony of the European Defence Community ended in disaster when the French Assembly refused to ratify the EDC Treaty in August 1954. Simultaneously there collapsed a number of abortive plans to set up a European Political Authority and other functional agencies. Some of the enthusiasts tried to revive the European movement at the Messina Conference in 1955, but there are few grounds for believing they will succeed.

There are two main reasons why the movement towards European federation collapsed. In the first place, when it came to the point, governments were unable to persuade their peoples to surrender total control of vital elements in their national strength. The fact that the French Assembly later accepted the Paris Treaties which involved the creation of a German national army suggests that it was the abolition of the French national army rather than the rearmament of Germans which decided the fate of EDC.

In the second place the fusion of nation states into a new

supranational organisation does not in itself abolish national disagreements or change the balance of power among the states concerned. Thus a people's attitude towards a new supranational organisation will depend as much on its proposed membership as on its proposed powers. For once the new organisation exists, its members cannot redress a balance of power they may dislike by calling on support from countries outside the group. That is one essential characteristic which distinguishes supranational from intergovernmental organisations. In the case of the European movement, it was Germany's inevitable predominance in a purely continental organisation which sealed its doom. It was useless to ask, as so many did, that Britain should join the movement as a counterpoise to Germany. For in doing so Britain in turn would lose her freedom to pursue her own major interests in cooperation with the Commonwealth and the U.S.A.

If the balance of power in a supranational organisation is unsatisfactory to one of its members, the existing conflict will be aggravated by the fact that a general surrender of sovereignty over a whole function of government compels the hostile parties to work together over a wide range of problems where they may have no common interest in cooperation. When two countries like France and Germany have been bad neighbours for so long, the worst way to solve their differences is to force them to get married and eat breakfast together till death do them part. Americans who cite their own history as an argument for federation tend to remember only the Act of Union. They forget the Civil War, in which they lost more men than in both of the World Wars which followed. Yet the Civil War was fought between two halves of a federal American Defence Community. The American Republic as we know it today was brought into being not by political consent but by military conquest.

The problem of membership is no less important for supranational organisations in the purely economic field, like a customs union, which in effect denies national governments an important element of fiscal freedom in relation to members of the group, and sets up new barriers between the group and countries outside it. The economic value of a European customs union does not depend simply on the fact that it creates a large single market—an exaggerated argument in any case, when the two most efficient European economies, the Swiss and the Swedish, have tiny internal markets. It depends also on the ability of its members to complement one another's deficiencies, but unfortunately the European economies are largely competitive rather than complementary. And it depends also on the type of competition which they provide for one another, compared with the competition which would otherwise come from outside the area. In too many fields the European countries have soft high cost economies. By creating a European preference at the expense of more vigorous competition from the U.S.A. and elsewhere, a customs union or single market might actually make Europe's economic problems worse, not better.

These general arguments are not necessarily valid against all proposals which have been or may be made for supranational authorities in Europe. In any case, a purely functional authority can rarely afford to use its supranational powers in practice unless it is backed by a federal government. In its early stages, the Schuman Plan worked because most of the sacrifices it demanded fell on German industry, and the German Government under Adenauer was prepared to punish industries which disobeyed the Authority's orders. Once a national government is unwilling to impose sanctions on recalcitrant businessmen, the Authority is powerless, for it has very few sanctions of its own to impose, beyond the withholding of dollar investment. In fact, it is doubtful whether for the last few years the Schuman Authority has invoked its supranational powers; it has sought instead to obtain consent for its proposals by the normal methods of consultation between the interests affected. Thus the sharp contrast which French and British politicians have so often drawn between supranational and intergovernmental agencies may well have little substance in practice. The juridical obstacles seen by both sides to closer British cooperation with the Continent may well be far less important than the practical arguments for such cooperation.

Besides the arguments from Europe's own interest against the federal approach to unity, there are powerful arguments from the viewpoint of countries outside Europe. Any new grouping tends to emphasise its internal cohesion only at the expense of its relations with those outside. For example, the creation of a single continental market would mean giving Germany a European preference at the expense of her main competitor, Britain. Many supporters of European federation have been inspired by the belief that this would produce a 'third force' between America and Russia, powerful enough to be independent of both. Others have seen federation as giving Europe a chance to re-assert its hegemony in Africa and Asia at a time when no European country by itself is strong enough to stem the anti-imperialist tide. Others again see it as offering the prospect of permanent discrimination against the dollar area. In fact there is a danger that any limited supranational grouping, far from marking a step towards world society, may render the basic problem of power politics even less tractable by creating a new and more formidable centre of independent power.

After this glance at the weaknesses and dangers of the juridical approach it is encouraging to turn to the patient empiricism of the organic approach as exemplified in some of the post-war intergovernmental organisations. The most striking gains in international unity since the war have been made through co-operation between governments depending on general consent. The achievements of the Organisation for European Economic Cooperation, though it depends on general agreement between sixteen independent governments, far excel those of the 'supranational' Schuman Plan. The members of OEEC have eliminated quantitative restrictions on 90 per cent of intra-European imports. By creating the European Payments Union in 1950 they made European currencies mutually convertible, and since the sterling area as a whole participates in EPU through Britain the EPU system covers well over half of all international transactions. As a result, the volume of intra-European trade has risen from a 1948 level 25 per cent below pre-war to a 1954 level 65 per cent above pre-war—with striking effects on employment and prosperity throughout the area. It should be stressed that America and Canada also participate in making the decisions of OEEC, and the danger of undue discrimination against the dollar area is thereby reduced.

In south east Asia the Colombo Plan has achieved results which are only a little less impressive than those of OEEC—again through free cooperation between governments. Starting with the Commonwealth countries alone—minus South Africa —the organisation later took in the other countries of south and east Asia as well as the United States. It has supervised the investment of thousands of millions of pounds, obtaining both money and technical assistance on a large scale from outside the area. Though its members disagree profoundly on many political questions, their economic cooperation has been smooth and fruitful.

In the political field the North Atlantic Treaty Organisation is the most interesting of all intergovernmental bodies. Despite its name it is not, essentially, a regional organisation. Although the commitment to collective military action covers only attacks on a member in a strictly defined area, there is no geographical limit to the area for which political and economic cooperation is envisaged; in recent years the Council has regularly exchanged views on the world situation as a whole.

One reason for the importance of NATO is that it is the only international organisation which exerts a major influence over the behaviour of the most powerful of all non-communist states —the U.S.A. Quite apart from the many arguments of narrow national interest which commit Britain to partnership with the U.S.A., there is an overwhelming general case for involving America as intimately as possible in international cooperation. Post-war developments have given America a vital national interest in events beyond the Atlantic and Pacific Oceans. No influential American any longer believes that his country can sit tight in hemispheric isolation. As recent events have underlined so forcibly, America's only alternative to international cooperation at present is not isolationism but 'going it alone'. It is a remarkable testimony to the basic idealism and good sense of the American people that they should not only have rejected this alternative but should have pursued cooperation with so emphatic a reliance on consent rather than force as the basis of their relations with those who in fact depend on them. Even when America has tied strings to her economic aid she has been reluctant to use economic sanctions to compel obedience. Denmark was allowed to send ships to Poland despite the fact that she had signed an agreement explicitly promising she would not do so.

NATO provides a fascinating example of the opportunities and limitations of intergovernmental cooperation. It started in 1949 by admitting that none of its members could build an adequate defence force on its own. Its aim therefore was to produce a balanced international defence force by requiring each member to specialise in the type of forces and arms for which it was best fitted. The aftermath of Korea, combined with political changes on both sides of the Atlantic, weakened the initial impetus, and it must be admitted that, beyond the impressive though still inadequate build-up in military strength, political and economic cooperation has recently fallen far short of the hopes of the Bevin-Truman period. And as emphasis on the thermo-nuclear deterrent has increased, there has been an alarming tendency in all NATO countries to abandon the attempt to build international defence forces in favour of national atomic striking power.

Since the continental members of NATO have failed to make an adequate contribution to the combined land armies, the real function of NATO has been quite different from that conceived by its founders. It has deterred aggression in Europe not by building the capacity to halt such aggression, but by committing the American Strategic Air Command—which is not itself under NATO control—to massive retaliation against Soviet cities if the Red Army were to move west. Because it is still insufficient to halt the Red Army, all the expensive paraphernalia of ground forces so far painfully amassed serves for little more than a burglar alarm or trip-wire to unleash the SAC.

Yet as Russia develops the power to retaliate in kind by thermo-nuclear attack on American cities, the Europeans are losing confidence in America's readiness to make the supreme sacrifice on their behalf. And instead of reviving the drive for collective land defence they are toying with the idea of acquiring their own thermo-nuclear deterrents. In fact modern weapons have made independent national defence a chimera. No state on earth can organise a deterrent against a rival which has thermo-nuclear striking power, except in cooperation with others. The power to deter atomic aggression depends on the capacity to retaliate in kind even after the aggressor has struck the first blow. This capacity in turn depends on the dispersal of atomic bases on an intercontinental scale. Even the United States itself with its mobile fleet carriers is incapable of sufficient dispersal of bases on its own. And since no foreign government is prepared to accept American air bases unless America helps to defend them against occupation by the Red Army, America was committed in her own military interest to help in the defence of western Europe even at a time when she had a virtual monopoly of atomic striking power. Though the advent of intercontinental missiles may modify this situation, it will not transform it altogether.

For smaller countries this is all the more true. For them, the cost of modern weapons excludes the building of an independent nuclear striking force to act as a deterrent. And as the great powers become more vulnerable to atomic attack themselves, a small power cannot rely on their protection unless it is prepared to join them in advance in organising a collective defence. The calculated risk of neutrality is bound to become less and less acceptable for a small power which is accessible to aggression.

Once states join to organise a common defence, they are involved in types of cooperation which create lasting interdependence. For example, since in NATO America has almost a monopoly of nuclear striking power, the other states depend absolutely on America for their deterrent to major aggression. On the other hand America's nuclear striking power still depends to a decisive extent on bases which her European allies control. This was one reason why in 1951, even if Truman had wished to take MacArthur's advice, he would have been unable to do so without the agreement of the other NATO powers. And it was one reason for the outcry in 1955 against Dulles' boast that Eisenhower had twice threatened to use atomic weapons in the Far East without informing America's European allies.

Though military cooperation is usually depreciated by idealists, it may sometimes be the surest means to creating an international community. For it involves to some degree a pooling of the most fundamental of all types of political power—physical force. The real complaint to be made against present military cooperation in NATO is that it falls far short of what the accepted interests of its members should dictate. Though, at least in the European area, none of the NATO powers can afford to consider independent military action, they have failed to take full advantage of their interdependence so as to increase their security and decrease their expenditure. Because America withholds her Strategic Air Command from NATO control, Britain has felt it necessary to spend millions on a thermo-nuclear deterrent of her own. And though in disarmament talks, Britain and America regularly protest their readiness to share their most intimate defence secrets with the Soviet Union, they refuse one another and their allies even the most elementary knowledge of their latest weapons. In consequence the NATO countries exhaust themselves in duplicating one another's efforts without achieving their most fundamental aim—the ability to halt the Red Army on the ground in Europe.

This is a dangerous weakness at the very heart of NATO. Until it is remedied, NATO's real achievements in international cooperation will be in jeopardy. Yet the very experience of working together for a common purpose has already done much to modify earlier patterns of national behaviour. For example, the so-called 'infrastructure' programme is something quite new in peacetime history. A network of bases and supply lines has been built up all over western Europe at a cost of over £700 million. In four years the number of military airfields was increased from 15 to 165.

If two states have an interest in working together on one issue, they have an interest in avoiding conflict on other issues which might damage such cooperation. Thus an interest in cooperation for even limited purposes creates an interest in consultation in a much wider field. The NATO interest in European defence promoted a discussion of France's problems in Indo-China, and should also promote discussion of Britain's problems in Cyprus. Such consultation may not lead to common policies in the wider field—but it at least gives governments the opportunity for choosing policies which are compatible with those of their friends. Conflicts of policy are due as often to ignorance as to intent. Though after consultation governments will not necessarily agree, at least they will not disagree unless necessary.

Over a period of time, cooperation and consultation is likely to lead to a new relationship between the states concerned —something almost justifying the word 'integration'. The individuals concerned at both the ministerial and departmental level develop habits of working together which are increasingly hard to break. And they develop a vested interest in cooperation which may survive changes in the circumstances which originally brought them together. In fact the countries in the group become increasingly interdependent.

Thus, though limited in their membership and functions, organisations such as NATO, OEEC and the Colombo Plan make an indispensable contribution towards the development of an international society. They provide the social tissue without which a sense of international community cannot survive the pressure of national interests. And they exert an influence over the behaviour of nation states which does limit in various degrees their ability as well as their desire to use their power for purely selfish ends.

The supreme advantage of the intergovernmental method is that it is less likely to produce the type of closed international society which simply raises the traditional problems of power politics to a new and more dangerous level. By its very nature the supranational or federal group creates new divisions in the world as a whole even as it removes divisions among its own members. At this particular point in history the most dangerous threat to peace would be too sharp a crystallisation of the obvious division between the rich white peoples of the Atlantic basin and the poor coloured peoples of Africa and Asia. Each group stands to lose immensely by emphasising the things which unite it internally as a community of culture instead of the things which unite it externally with mankind as a whole.

The intergovernmental method tends to discourage closed international groupings. By choosing its partners according to the specific interests it wishes to promote, a state can spread its roots far and wide throughout the world, and act as a link between other states which have no direct contact. For example, Britain's dual role as a member both of NATO and of the Commonwealth has enabled her to bring Indian and American views on Asia closer together. Similarly India's contacts with the west through the Commonwealth and with the Soviet bloc through the Bandoeng Conference have helped her to play a constructive role in the cold war. Of course, commitment to one group for one function is liable to exclude a commitment to a rival or hostile group with the same function—but it does not exclude commitments to countries which are not hostile even for the same function. Britain's military commitment to NATO does not exclude her from fulfilling quite different military responsibilities inside the Commonwealth. Doubt whether EDC would have left France a similar freedom was a major reason for its rejection by the French Assembly.

At first sight the untidy complex mass of overlapping international organisations cries out for pruning and rationalisation. Yet a closer study will usually show that something immensely valuable would be sacrificed by such a tidying up. For example, there was a move a few years ago to let NATO take over OEEC since the membership of the two bodies was almost identical. Almost, but not quite. And in fact NATO would have lost as much through the exclusion of the neutral countries from Atlantic economic cooperation as Sweden, Switzerland and Austria themselves. In fact this untidy proliferation of international tissue provides a much tougher and more resilient basis for world order than an artificial symmetry.

The objection is often made that cooperation between governments cannot provide an absolute guarantee against secession. The interests which originally stimulated cooperation may change, or governments may come to power which take a different view of those interests. At most cooperation over a period may accumulate a number of marginal disincentives against a breakaway. Only statesmanship and good fortune can ensure that the group is not subjected to strains powerful enough to overcome such disincentives.

All this is true enough. Yet on balance it constitutes yet another argument in favour of the intergovernmental approach. Even supranational institutions allow the possibility of secession in practice though they deny it in theory. They simply ensure that if secession takes place, it inflicts far more damage on other members of the group. And by enforcing uniformity in fields where those concerned might well differ without harming the common interests of the group, they narrow the field within which statesmanship can avoid dangerous strains.

In fact the intergovernmental approach is far better suited to allow the adjustments which a changing situation makes desirable. And since this is above all an age of change, flexibility is an essential element in any international organisation. Any approach to world order must allow the possibility of peaceful change—what Jaspers has called the possibility of continuous self-rectification through the voluntary renunciation of power, both by members of the group and by the group as a whole. This is indeed one aspect of the eternal conflict between freedom and authority. And it is a powerful argument against the juridical approach to international organisation. A social order must reflect the existing pattern of power relations among its component parts; but it must also be capable of adaptation to any change in that pattern. A closed supranational grouping carries real dangers in this respect. Besides setting rigid limits to the freedom of its members to associate with others outside the group, its juridical constitution is bound to reflect too faithfully the relations between its members at the moment of its foundation. For example, the European Defence Community was originally conceived by France as a means of controlling Germany's revival. But in the interval between its conception in 1949 and its completion in 1952, Western Germany had already recovered so much strength that EDC was more likely to be dominated by Germany than to control Germany. And after its rejection by France in 1954, Germany herself had developed so many interests outside Europe that she had become reluctant to confine herself too narrowly inside a single continent.

Today the major unsolved problem in Europe is that of German reunification. A supranational link between the Federal Republic and her western neighbours would create so direct and obvious a conflict between German reunification and European Union that Bonn's cooperation with the west would be subjected to dangerous strains. The present system by which Bonn is associated with NATO leaves a latitude for negotiation with Russia which is essential whether or not German unity can ultimately be achieved.

In the world as a whole the major problem is to construct a system which will permit the Asian and African peoples to carry through their double revolution against poverty and white control without coming into conflict with the richer white nations.

Here the danger of too rigid a pattern of association between Asia and the west is more obvious still. Only the loosest framework of relations is likely to survive the gigantic political, social, and economic changes through which Asia is passing. It is essential to avoid pressing diplomacy into a rigid mould which later developments are bound to crack.

It may be dangerous to snatch temporary opportunities for tying Asian countries into military alliances with the west if the general trend of their development is in a contrary direction. In the economic field, some well-meaning western proposals assume a willingness in the Asian countries to accept a type of external direction and control which is bound in time to appear as imperialism in a new dress. And in general, the sense of a common Asian unity *vis à vis* the white countries is so important a factor that the advantages the west might gain through special associations with particular Asian countries must be weighed against the possible damage to a wider *entente* with Asia as a whole, if such associations are resented outside the countries concerned.

In fact the transition from a polity of power to a polity of consent based on international order poses difficult problems of judgment at every stage. The dynamics of power politics continue to function during the evolution of a system which is intended ultimately to transcend them. Just as in the mixed economy typical of a democratic transition to socialism the laws of capitalist development continue to apply so far as the profit motive influences economic behaviour, so, even while governments are trying to construct a new international polity by collective action, their behaviour remains governed to a large extent by their conception of their national interests and by the physical power which they can mobilise to secure those interests. Different states, or different parties within each state, may legitimately differ in their analysis of a situation, in the priority they give to the national and international strands in their policy, in preferring a larger community at the expense of closer integration, or vice versa. Often the most difficult choice of all is between the use of power and the pursuit of consent when the ultimate aims of the other party are uncertain—British Guiana and the Suez base provide interesting examples.

Where general principles provide so inadequate a guide for specific judgments, everything depends on the government having at least a strong sense of direction, and on the people's general readiness to make sacrifices for the sake of international cooperation. It is here that the differences of moral predilection on which political parties are based may lead to differences in foreign policy—though in practice an intelligent view of national interest may lead a Conservative towards international cooperation or a parochial view of socialist doctrine may lead a Labour politician in the opposite direction.

Whatever the difficulties of judgment at the governmental level, there is still a formidable task for individuals and organisations to do in educating public opinion on the need for international cooperation and in encouraging the moral qualities required to sustain it. Against the background of earlier periods, public opinion in this generation has shown an astonishing readiness to make sacrifices for wider ends than the nation state. It is, for example, quite remarkable that the American people, which twenty years ago committed itself by law to isolationism, should in the last eight years have paid in taxation over forty billion dollars—a thousand dollars a family—to finance help to other peoples, and that half of that help should have been economic with no direct benefit to America's military security.

Yet even now neither governments nor peoples seem fully aware of the urgency of developing closer international unity. It is just becoming apparent that unless greater progress is made quickly, both the military and the peaceful uses of nuclear energy will make the problem much more difficult. On the military side, failures in cooperation between allies are driving one country after another into producing for itself the most destructive of all atomic weapons. The American monopoly has already been broken by Russia and Britain. Within ten years every big industrial power may have followed suit, together with some smaller powers like Sweden. If this process continues it will not only disrupt the existing military alliances but make it much more difficult to create new ones. The resulting diplomatic instability is terrifying to contemplate.

This problem is complicated by the fact that there is no means of producing atomic energy for industrial purposes which does not carry with it the power to make nuclear weapons. A close international control of atomic power plants is essential to the control of atomic weapons. Yet at present Britain and America are sacrificing the chance to establish such control for the sake of preserving a five year lead in their national atomic programmes. Even in the strictly economic field atomic energy poses urgent diplomatic problems. The comparatively wealthy European countries cannot produce atomic energy economically without a degree of cooperation among themselves far more intimate than they have achieved in the Coal and Steel Pool. The underdeveloped areas in Asia and Africa which need atomic energy most cannot hope to produce it on a large scale without tremendous financial assistance from Europe and America. And even when the power plants exist, they will be useless until the machines and factories they are to drive are also there; this too will demand large-scale external aid. In other words, atomic power will still further widen the gulf in living standards and productivity between Asia and the west, until the west takes action to prevent this. Unless a major redistribution of the world's income takes place soon, there will be little chance of obtaining Asian and African cooperation in building a world society. Because the military use of atomic power reduces the gap between rich and poor states while the industrial use of atomic power may well increase it, poor states with large populations may be tempted to concentrate on the former unless they are given an incentive to do otherwise.

This is one of the many reasons why the communist leaders show so much confidence in their own ultimate triumph, and so little interest in pursuing the democratic approach to international order. Both in their words and in their deeds the Soviet leaders have made it all too clear that they believe non-communist states are unable to solve their internal contradictions, and that the world can be united only through the expansion of their own system, which is historically inevitable.

There are grounds for believing that circumstances may melt the present rigidity of communist international doctrine, and undermine Russia's present confidence. Already the existence of independent communist parties in China and Yugoslavia has compelled Khrushchev to surrender the total authority which

Stalin once exercised within the communist world. Sooner or later the latent conflicts between rival Communist Parties may erupt as conflicts between the states they rule.

But the only sure basis for long-term optimism depends on the success of the non-communist countries in mastering the conflicts among themselves. For if we refuse to verify communist predictions of our disintegration, we shall not only be immune to further communist pressure, we shall also shake the doctrinal certainty which communist experience in the first forty years since the October Revolution has done more to confirm than to weaken. Only then will the communists have any real incentive to modify their opinions and their policies.

For the time being the communist bloc provides the rest of the world with just one more argument for transcending its own international anarchy. In fact, this may prove the strongest argument of all. Fear is unfortunately still the most potent stimulus to international action, and a visible danger inspires a livelier reaction than a theoretical argument. In the days when herrings were carried back alive to harbour from the fishing grounds, nearly a third were liable to die on the long journey. Finally the fishermen solved the problem by putting a dogfish in the herring hold. Though it might eat hundreds, it saved the lives of thousands more by keeping them on the move. Professor Toynbee may well be right in predicting that future historians will see communism as playing an indispensable role in the twentieth century—as the dogfish in the tank of herring.